Short and Sweet too

Connie Inglis pg 73

Joy Bailey pg. 63

Carol Schafer pg. 22

Lynn Dove p. 58

More Small Words for Big Thoughts

Still Warm

Still Wise

Still Witty

COMPILED AND EDITED BY

SUSAN CHEEVES KING

GRACE
PUBLISHING

BROKEN ARROW, OK

Royalties for this book are donated to World Christian Broadcasting.

SHORT AND SWEET TOO
More Small Words for Big Thoughts:
Still Warm, Still, Wise, Still Witty

ISBN-13: 978-1-60495-031-1

DEDICATION

To God to whose service I dedicate my life
and to my dear, sweet husband, Joe,
who supports me in everything I do for Him.

ACKNOWLEDGEMENTS

To all the writers who practice their craft day after day
without ever being acknowledged.

TABLE OF CONTENTS

INTRODUCTION

It all started decades ago when Mary Lou Redding (pp. 88-89) caught an idea from a professor at Fort Wayne University. Further inspired by Joseph A. Ecclesine's "Big Words Are for the Birds" (at the end of the Introduction), she started assigning a one-syllable-word exercise in classes she taught at various writers' conferences all over the country.

Over the past twenty years, I have continued giving this assignment to those in my own classes. Writers at these conferences are motivated to learn whatever I can teach them about perfecting their craft because they know they're going to apply what they've learned, probably within an hour after they leave the classroom.

Still, they have come with the attitude that we who love to write all share. After all, we're writers. We love words. If a few words are good, many are better — especially the interesting word, maybe the elegant word…and definitely the special word only a particular writer can use.

And we do love to use the long, impressive words. But that can work against good communication. The truth is, the best communication is what the readers/listeners understand with the least effort — a Mr. Spock mind meld as it were — as if the ideas are just flowing from the writer's mind to theirs with no actual words involved.

We may love words, but if we use too many of them and ones that are not familiar and comfortable to the average reader/listener, then words just get in the way. Writing tight (saying a lot with a little) and using crisp, clear, accessible words in our writing and speech bring joy to the readers/listeners even if they may not know why.

That's good news for any of us who long for others to understand us, to hear us. The words we really should be using most of the time are already known to us. We don't have to get a college degree to learn them; we just think that we do. So we all need to break our attachments to those multi-syllable aliens that even non-professional writers/speakers tend to favor and get back to the simple words of our childhood.

Here is the assignment the writers in this book were given:

Choose something you are passionate about, something that's important to you. Write about it in 200-275 words, using words of only one syllable. Fiction, non-fiction, and poetry pieces are eligible. Exceptions:

- Any proper noun is okay. (Don't lie. If you were born in *California*, don't write *Maine*; if a name is *Machenheimer*, don't write *Clark*.)
- You may use multisyllabic words of five letters or fewer — *area, about.*
- You may use contractions of more than one syllable — *didn't.*
- You may use numbers (even those that are multisyllabic).
- You may quote the Bible word-for-word.

If you're a writer — or aspire to be — and this assignment intrigues you, why not give it a try and then email what you've written to shortandsweet@gmail.com? You could be seeing your own work featured in an upcoming book in the Short and Sweet series.

- Susan Cheeves King

BIG WORDS ARE FOR THE BIRDS

Joseph A. Ecclesine

When you come right down to it, there is no law that says you have to use big words in ads.

There are lots of small words, and good ones, that can be made to say all the things you want to say — quite as well as the big ones.

It may take more time to find the small words — but it can be well worth it. For most small words are quick to grasp. And best of all, most of us know what they mean.

Some small words — a lot of them, in fact — can say a thing just the way it should be said. They can be crisp, brief, to the point. Or they can be soft, round, smooth — rich with just the right feel, the right taste.

Use them with care and what you say can be slow or fast to read — as you wish.

Small words have a charm all their own — the charm of the quick, the lean, the lithe, the light on their toes. They dance, twist, turn, sing — light the way for the eyes of those who read, like sparks in the night — and stay on to sing some more.

Small words are clean, the grace notes of prose. There is an air to them that leaves you with the keen sense that they could not be more clear.

You know what they say the way you know a day is bright and fair — at first sight. And you find as you read that you like the way they say it.

Small words are sweet — to the ear, the tongue, and the mind.

Small words are gay — and lure you to their song as the flame lures the moth (which is not a bad thing for an ad to do).

Small words have a world of their own — a big world in which all of us live most of the time (which makes it a good place for ads, too).

And small words can catch big thoughts and hold them up for all who read to see — like bright stones in rings of gold.

With a good stock of small words, and the will to use them, you can write ads that will do all you want your ads to do — and more, much more.

In fact, if you play your cards right, you can write ads the way they all say ads should be done: in words like these (all the way down to the last one, that, is) of just one syllable.

About Joseph A. Ecclesine

Joseph A. Ecclesine was a Madison Avenue copywriter in the *Mad Men* era. He originally wrote this piece in the 1960s for other copywriters."

A shorter version titled "Words of One Syllable," ran in *Reader's Digest*.

These two versions have also appeared in various other publications while being used as inspirational models for college writing courses around the country.

Born in Boston, Ecclesine graduated from Fordham University in 1929, months before the stock market crash that triggered the Great Depression. He was fortunate to find work at the *Bronx Home News* during that period. He later worked in the press department of NBC in Manhattan, where he met his future wife, Margy, also a writer there.

They celebrated more than 50 years of marriage and had eight children. While living in New York, he worked at several major ad agencies and became promotion director of *Look Magazine*.

His catchy headlines and prose could be found in the campaigns of numerous companies, including IBM, National Geographic, Revlon and American Airlines. He also wrote fiction and essays, with a 1930s piece in *Esquire* magazine, followed by work in *The New Yorker, Newsweek* and *Short Story International*. He had an innate curiosity about everything, which translated into an extreme zest for life.

An accomplished watercolorist, Ecclesine allegedly sold his first piece to boxer Gene Tunney, who held the world heavyweight championship in the late 1920s. Ecclesine's watercolors were featured in *The Artist* magazine, and he had a one-man show during his retirement in San Diego. While living in California during his final years, he taught courses in memoir writing for senior citizens in a continuing education program at UCSD (University of California at San Diego).

1

SMALL WORDS, DEEP THOUGHTS

You said to write a piece that used only small words. Well, that's dumb. You can't write deep thoughts with tiny words. How can you write a grand or fine or rich idea with such wee words? You can't.

So I won't do it. I quit. And just to show you, I'm going to break the rules. I'll write on all the stuff I think is deep — too deep for small words, too big for plain, short blurts like sound bites. I'll use the kind of big, long words that you find in fat, grey books, bound in dust at the backs of shelves. I'll use words that make your eyes pop, that make your brain steam.

You see, I want to talk of what is true, most true — so thick and real and must-know that you don't dare go out while blind to it. I want to talk of what is right there in front of you that the eyes in your face can't see but that the eye in your heart sees and sees so clear, sees right through — if you could just learn to let your heart see and not let your hand get in the way.

There seems to be so much of that: the dark light which God hid in things we can't *not* see. God has put it just out of reach so that we have to lean, to stretch, to hold out empty hands, to search, to long, and then at last to find. That holy stuff all lies right here and waits for us. And when we see, it's as if a new dawn has come, and we hold it to our hearts and walk out into the light.

All of that is in the world and in our hearts. And the one small door that lets us bring those gems out to the light, the thin bridge that helps us bring them to our friends and show them, is our words: these frail things that all are much too weak to bear the weight of truth, too dumb to hold the vast, dense flesh of God that haunts this world.

So in the end we all are stumped by this fool's task. No words at all, short or long, can bring us close to God — none but the least of them, the most plain and clear as glass, like "here" or "now," like "I" and "you" and "we," like "Wow." Like, "Ah."

Steve Garnaas-Holmes

2
THE TOUCH THAT HEALS

A mom's hands touch her child
for the first time
as new life cries out.

I rub Dad's feet with oil
while he lies still
and quiet
on the bed.
God will take him home soon.

No words.
Just skin on skin.
An act of love.
God's love in the flesh.

From birth to death, touch says,
"I care.
I see you.
I want to help.
I hurt with you.
It's safe now to let go.
Just relax and rest."

Touch is still my job,
though I thought I gave it up.

Now I ask,
Do the words I speak and write
touch hearts
and minds
and souls
the way my hands have done
over the years?

"Yes," God says, "if you let me guide them."
Linda Jett

3

TO BE REAL

It was planned for my grant team to do an on-site check at a state jail. About four days from our visit, we got an email that the jail was on "lock down" — all visits banned. I hate to admit this, but I was glad. I know that Jesus said "*I was in prison and you came to visit me,*" (in Matt. 25:36 NIV), but I was scared to go.

Less than a day later, we got an email that the visit was back on. *Nuts*! I would go, but I was full of fear.

The man who sat next to me in that room had a tear tat on his cheek. "I killed a man," he groaned and stared right at me. "And I am sorry. I wasn't sorry then, but I am now. Jesus saves."

Each man there shared that he had shot to kill to be part of a gang. They talked about how they joined gun-and-rage gang raids, just so they would fit in. And, while in this jail — in these cells with no way out — they had come to grasp that the only one they should care about was a dude named Jesus Christ who loved them so very much.

At the base of what these men had done was the wish to be liked.

Just like me — and maybe, you.

We fear what this one or that one will think of us. We fear that we will seek help and no one will come. We fear that we will be laughed at. Or that our pure-white coat will show its spots.

If we could shed this white cloak of fear and "know the truth" about each other —with its real spots and scars — I know that others would also shed their cloaks and be "real." And soon, the truth would "set us free" (John 8:32) and all cloaks would be gone.

We could zap fear in its tracks. With a gun of truth.

When I strive to act as if all is okay, (when it is not), I think back to that room and those men. They were *so* real that day.

And I see that if guys in a jail can be real, then so can I. With God's help, I can tell the good (and the bad) about me and my life and still be *sure* of His — and your — love for me, for truly, Jesus has the final say. He can break the lock on every cell.

Anne F. Rauth

4

THEOPHELIA

Be imitators of God, as dearly loved children. And walk in love, as the Messiah also loved us, a sacrificial and fragrant offering to God.

Ephesians 5:1-2 HCSB

Her name is Theophelia, and she is from Guana. That's what it says on the Compassion International card. On a table at the back of our church many of these cards — each with a child's image — lie in neat, even rows. I scan each card until Theophelia's draws me in. The dark eyes that fill her face are void of hope or life. And the dress she wears hangs off her frame as if she were a frail tree with a lank trunk and limbs so thin that I doubt they could bear the weight of even one small bird. The dress might fit a ten-year-old, but Theophelia is only four. She wears no shoes. She wears no smile.

Through the noise of the church crowd, I hear that soft inner voice I've grown to know — "She is the child you've prayed for." I pick up Theophelia's card and sign my name along the thin black line. I will not need to give up much for this child to gain much. Soon this child will have food. Soon she will have clothes that fit. Soon she will learn of our one true God — the God who will bring her hope. It won't be long and Theophelia's dark eyes will shine.

Wendy Dunham

Note: Compassion International is a child-advocacy ministry that pairs compassionate people with children in poverty.

5
ONE OF A KIND

My spouse and I left the cold and snow to spend a week in Mexico. Our plan for this trip was to sit in the sun and soak up the heat.

Each day we went for a long walk on the beach. The waves would lap at our feet, and the calm shore filled us with peace. Most days the sky was clear blue with a few wisps of white clouds. The sun would heat us up, and then a soft breeze from the sea would blow in to cool us back down. As we walked, we searched for shells to take home with us.

One day I bent to pick up a shell but then left it on the sand. It did not fit in with the other ones I sought. That's when I felt God speak to me. "My child," He said, "you are like this shell. I love you just as you are and don't want you to try to be the same as the rest. Be proud of who you are. I didn't make you to be usual or the norm."

I was in awe to know that God would use this trip to speak right to my heart. He led me to the shells on the beach to teach me that I am blessed to be one of a kind in His sight.

Tandy Balson

6

MOOSE

My nine-year-old dog, Moose, is dark brown and weighs eleven pounds. I'm glad that he's small since he likes to sleep on top of my legs or curl up next to me in bed. He's the apple of

MOOSE

my eye, and to me, he can all but walk on water. My one gripe is that once in a blue moon, he shreds paper and leaves chaos on the floor.

Using a deep voice, I scold, "Moose, you know Mama doesn't like this. You are not a billy goat." But in fact, I don't care since this kind of mess takes a flash to clean up. I act upset so that he doesn't find a new way to defy the rules.

All forms of life must have the deep urge to rebel in some way, and I'm on cloud nine that at least he doesn't eat shoes or bite folks.

I love his zeal. When I enter a room, he wags his tail or barks with gusto when I come back home. He will pivot his small head back and forth when I talk to him, as if he wants to grasp every word. That is more than I can say for my sons or their boys.

A friend calls him *Bullet* since he runs like the wind to chase a ball. And when he gives a fist bump with his tiny paw, it's just too cute.

Of course, I miss him when I'm away. Then I walk through the door, and see his sweet brown eyes and feel his licks on my face — and I start to love him all over again. Even if I see a pile of paper shreds on the floor.

Tammy Van Gils

7

THE FILTH-PIT TAMER

AARGH! I can't stand this filth pit one more day!"

That lady's heart cry is one I've heard many times over the years. That's why I love to help folks get junk-free.

Some items are needs. Ask any mom with a wet baby. Extra child-care items are needs. Fifty stuffed toys aren't.

What kinds of things fill, sometimes stuff, our homes? Clothes we can't wear, books we don't read, and piles of paper we don't need, to name a few.

Why is it so hard to let go of things?

The Bible tells us death and the grave are never satisfied, and neither are we (Prov. 27:20 CEV).

But folks can stop the hold-and-hoard cycle. How do I help bring a home's chaos into order? Each time I aid a man or lady, the first thing we do is pray. Then we move through their house and sort through things. Good items stay. The rest goes.

For those who want to keep too many items, I ask, "Who could you bless with this?" That phrase sets folks free. Their thoughts change from, "Where can I put all this stuff?" to "Who can I help with it?"

After the big purge, folks revel in their open space. They have fresh hope, and light hearts. When I see the glow on their faces, I feel that more than their homes were cleaned. It brings to mind Psalm 51:10: Create in me a clean heart, O God, and renew a right spirit within me. (ESV)

And the lady who was fed up with her "filth pit"? Like many before her, she gave all her extra things to those in need. As she puts it, "Now I'm free!"

Jeanie Jacobson

8
QUEST FOR THE TRUTH

God made me to crave the truth. I yearn for it. Like air for the lungs, it fills my soul and brings life. I long for it to wash me clean and make me pure. When I flow over with truth, then I can help friends find hope.

Here is what truth means to me. When Jesus says that He is the truth (John 14:6), this claim calls to mind a span from God to man, a long chain of pure strength that links God and man. Tough as nails, it rules like a king and fills our world with real facts that help us feel firm and sure. Christ is the truth with whom we will live when this age ends. These thoughts guide me in my quest for truth.

I find it odd that God lets us twist, change, and kill the truth just like Satan did to tempt Eve to eat the fruit of the Tree of the Knowledge of Good and Evil. But God gave us a choice, and that makes me feel that I should be alert in how I speak the truth. I must state the truth well, clear it of any error, and tell it clean. I get mad when man grinds the truth under his foot for I know that no good can come of it.

I love the truth with its stark black and white that points to the best way. It lights my path, shields me from harm and sets me free. God's Son *is* the truth, and my quest for Him never ends.

Marlene Houk

9
GOD'S GLOBE

Even though the frail globe rocked on its axis, I was still quite fond of it. Where it came from, I don't know. In our old farm home, needs were met, and love flowed deep; but we had no room for frills.

I loved the way the globe felt under my thumb, as it spun and swayed. One soft push, and I closed my eyes to dream of a place far away. I hoped to see the world one day. God's big world. I prayed to visit other spots, but the child's wish seemed in vain. Yet I prayed; I spun; I dreamed. The big world turned.

And God heard the thoughts of a small girl.

With a ring on my left hand, I trekked with my Navy love to Jacksonville. My world grew. Our base home sat a stone's throw from the St. John's River. I gained a stamp from Barbados and Quixto. I dunked in the ocean and gazed at the Andes Mountains.

Uncle Sam said, "Camp LeJeune," and then an Israel stamp came next. I ate a gyro, rode a camel. I saw an olive tree where my Savior might have sought shade. Virginia took us north. We touched Canada and saw New York and Niagara Falls and spots close by.

Our zip code changed to the west coast first in California and then in Washington. The Pacific Ocean cooled; Death Valley warmed, and Mt. St. Helen's thrilled.

The globe spun and my world grew. God heard the words of a small girl, and I learned to trust His words: Take delight in the LORD, and he will give you the desires of your heart. (Ps. 37:4 NIV)

Julie Lavender

10
JOY OF HEART

They will scarcely brood over the days of their lives,
because God keeps them occupied
with the joy of their hearts.

Ecclesiastes 5:20 NRSV

While there is much to care about in our world, I like to take time out to sit on my porch where I can view God's earth. When the sun shines (and where I live, it does not shine much of the year), the light beams through the trees and grants rest for my eyes. Green leaves seem to glow. Deep blue sky peeks through tree limbs. Birds sing. Blooms rise from the ground and brush the sky. Bugs fly their rounds. God gives joy to my heart.

As I sit, a great bird with a loud squawk lands in a tree next to the street. He tucks his huge wings. I see his hooked beak swing side to side as he shrieks and seems to judge those who do not heed. I watch as cars race by, folks jog with plugs in their ears, a man on a bike pumps his legs and huffs up the hill. But no one seems to care about the brash fowl in their midst.

I am so glad I am on my porch and have not missed this treat. The great bird lifts his wings and soars. I am sad for those who did not see or hear him. But oh! How blessed I am! God gave me eyes to see. My heart fills with joy through this grand gift.

Linda Jo Reed

11
MY MAN

I care about the man in my life. Bob's eyes look out for my best. His mouth speaks kind words over me, and his arms are firm and strong about me. My love is tough and wise. He likes to please me even when I might not merit it, and he can build things for our home. When we take a trip, he drives — but not like most men. If we get lost, he is quick to ask for help.

Susanna and Bob

Years ago, Bob fought fires: brush fires, house fires, and trash-can fires. But when there were no fires to put out, silly things took place at the fire house. Once, a man stood on top of the fire-house roof with a pail of water that he poured down all over the love of my life. It was the source of a good laugh for all. And Bob didn't seem to mind.

Alas, old thoughts live on, but my love's fire days have long since gone. The need to feel close to a group of men who work side by side left my man years ago. The surge of quick deeds to assist others is not a basic need for him now. But the love of my life still has a fire in him. He acts on the needs of the day just where he happens to be, at home or far off.

Bob lends a kind ear to other long-ago fire men whose hearts match his heart. My love still looks out for me. He likes to keep gas in the tank of my car. He makes sure to lock all the doors of our place at night. And my man doesn't seem to mind.

Susanna Robar

12

A Great Place to Buy Shoes

In Santa Maria, way up in Guatemala's hills, our team was to spend a day with kids in their school; but I had stayed back to clean the bus so was too late to meet them. While I sat on the school's steps, three boys joined me. We smiled back and forth, their dark eyes filled with awe. I must have seemed odd to them, and it seemed odd to me that they weren't in school.

I glanced at their feet and began to point first to my feet and then theirs. They looked down, shook their heads, and hid their toes in the dirt. I glanced over at the other kids in the yard. *Lord, does the fact that these boys have no shoes bar them from school?*

CAROL SHAFER WITH GUATEMALAN BOY

A wild urge to shop thrust me to my feet. "Come!" They came. "Come," I said to the friend who helped our team speak Spanish. We marched to the square where bright cloths were spread on the ground and found one with piles of shoes. My young friends stared, not sure what was going on, as I dropped to my knees to search for shoes to fit them.

"Come." I helped them slip shoes on their bare feet. They laughed and jumped, as boys do when life is fun! Sounds of joy filled the square as all who watched spoke of what they saw in words I didn't know.

"How much?" I asked the dazed man whose piles we'd just strewn. I pulled out bills and coins. He grinned with all the teeth he still had.

Oh, Jesus, life's such a blast when I can live this close to your heart!

Carol Schafer

13

THE ONE NEW MAN

In Ephesians 3:4-6, Paul wrote about "the mystery of Christ" — that *Gentiles are heirs together with Israel* (NIV), and that Jews who have faith in Jesus join Gentiles as one body in Him. Very few Jews go to our church so our friends did not mull over this key truth until my spouse, David, and I chose the "mystery of Christ" as a theme of our *Jewish Roots* Bible study. Then, our class began to focus on the scope of our unity in Christ.

This issue is close to my heart. When David first told me about Christ, I said, "Go find somebody to date in your Singles Class at church. I'm Jewish." David stuck it out to teach me about Jesus. He prayed again and again. In God's time, my mom, Uncle Louie, and I — all Jewish — chose Messiah Yeshua (Jesus) as Lord of our lives.

DEBORAH AND DAVID

My heart sings with joy when I share in class that we are joint heirs by faith in Christ. In Old Testament times, Gentiles were "far away" from God and Jews were "near" via the Law of Moses (Eph. 2:13-22). Now, we are equal in Him. We can praise God side by side. Ever since Jesus died on the cross and rose from the dead, God's heirs are all who have faith in Him. (See Gal. 3:28-29.) The shed blood of Christ saves us all.

Paul's two-fold life's work was done: *to preach to the Gentiles the boundless riches of Christ and to make plain to everyone the administration of this mystery* (Eph. 3:8-9) — the union of Jews and Gentiles in Christ, the sweet aroma of the Prince of Peace.

Deborah Brawer Silva

14
Interview with a Super Hero

A few years ago, I was in a food store where a woman was helping her aged father shop. I stopped to thank that man — since to me, he had saved the world.

He smiled and reached out a shaky hand to touch my arm. "I had a lot of help," he said.

What made me think that he'd saved the world?

Was I wrong about the part he played, that his story grew out of the midst of our shared story?

I knew to thank him by the image of a B-24 Liberator Bomber sewn on his hat. The sleek and cool B-17 Flying Fortress got more press, but the men in the B-24s flew more, bombed more, and fought more during World War II than their Boeing kin. Men in both did a lot of dying.

I used to stop and thank WWII vets often — when I saw the hat, lapel pin, or signs on their cars. We would share a few words and then shake hands. They'd say a name or place — The Marshall Islands, Anzio, Ploesti, The Hump. And I'd know it, from my love for the past and the way I yearn to know much about the land I adore.

They seemed to like that I knew the names of each place where they'd lost friends — or limbs.

These days I thank them less and less for I just don't see them very often. They are leaving this world for their final home at a rate of 400 per day.

Is it too much to say that these men are Super Heroes? Well, what does a Super Hero do?

Save the world.

That's what these men did so many years ago.

Jeff Brady

15
Not In Vain

My beloved brethren, be steadfast, immovable, always abounding in the work of the Lord, knowing that your toil is not in vain in the Lord.
1 Corinthians 15:58 NASB

When called upon to write a prayer book, I knew that Satan would strike. He taunts me when I toil for the Lord. So I prepped for the fight. Let the bout begin! God's on my side.

Round One: My kin asked my spouse, Tom, and me to join them for a week at the beach. I took Tom's Dell to write, but Word wouldn't open. I used pen and pad instead.

Score: Me – one; Satan – zip.

Round Two: A swarm of bugs took over our home. We moved out for three days, while a tent lay over our house. My pen and pad proved handy again.

Score: Me – two; Satan – zip.

My day job made me too tired to write. Round Three gained one for Satan. But later, time off to rest and write ripped that point back from my foe.

Score: Me – three; Satan – zip.

Two months later, my dear Tom passed into Heaven. I couldn't go on. Had I lost in Round Four?

Weighed down by grief, I cried out to the Lord, "I can't do this!"

"Of course, you can't," came God's soft reply. "Not on your own. What does My Word say?"

I wiped my tears. "*I can do all things through him who gives me strength*" (Phil. 4:13 NIV).

Janet and Tom

He rolled away the heavy stone from my heart.

As loved ones prayed for me, the Lord gave me peace; and His words flowed through me.

Score: **God** and me – four; Satan – zip.

Janet Ramsdell Rockey

16

THE MOM
TO CHANTEL (SEE FACING PAGE.)

Nine at night, on the day you were born, I could not have known how I'd love you. Then, there you were: with big blue eyes that lit up that day at the sound of my voice and still shine now when they see my face.

A child who smiles! You and I, we choose to smile each day. Did I teach you that or was it a thing you just knew how to do? How sweet that is — a gift from God to a mom.

But how would I care for this gift? I thought: *God trusts me with this child. How does He know I can do this?* But oh, yes, He knows I am young. He knows I'm not wise, so He stays by my side. He guides me through the hard times and through the joy, and we share the love of this child. For yes you love me, and yes you love God more, and I hope that He is as glad of that as I am.

TRISHA WITH DAUGHTER, CHANTEL MATHSON

I watch as you grow, and I see that I have taught you some good things, and I see that God shows you all the rest. And of course, He does it best so that in the end we can both be proud of who you are and who you have yet to be. I see you with my heart, and He sees in your soul — and so far we've done well, He and I.

Trisha Barry

I Can Do That, Too

Today, I see a small girl who wants to be just like her Mom. I was once just like that child. "Mom," I'd say, "you lead, you care, you laugh, you share," and soon I said (at first, to no one but me): "I can do that, too."

When I was small, you seemed so tall, and now I see that, at five foot three, you are not. But your heart is tall, and that is what my heart could see: you were (and still are) so tall to me. You speak, they clap, I like that — and soon, I guess: I can do that, too.

And so one day, I try my best. I speak, like you, and they hear me too, and they learn and they smile, and it heals some hearts. It's who we are, and soon I see: I can do that, too.

I watch you, Mom, and I see. It's how you are; it's how it should be; in fact, it's how I *will* be. You pray, so I pray. You give, so I give. You love, so I love. This is how God meant our lives to be: You show His ways to me. I learn them from you. And now it's up to me to pass it on to my kids, who will pass it on to their kids. And so the good work of the world goes on, and now I know: I am part of His plan — and I can do that, too.

Chantel Mathson

SOARING!

Poems are the clouds that float
Above the wide blue sky
And turn the tired eyes to see
The sun that shines on high;

Words bring sleep to those too glad
To close their misty eyes
And find the rest and sweet-sky hope
That grace, like dawn, will rise;

Words set hearts on once-far shores
And sing their songs to us the poor
And press their flights upon our minds
And give us space to breathe again;

Words are stars that light our ways,
Burn in thoughts through our long days,
Give us thrills — though often fleet —
And leave a touch of inner peace;

Words can raise our hearts like air,
Lift off the weight of chain-like fear
Give us proof that love will last
'Til our chores of life are past.

Words are but a trail of ink along a faded page;
But words can heal the heart and mind and sweep our doubts away.

Adrienne

19

WHY I LOVE DOGS

To tell the truth, I love dogs. It's not that I don't like cats; they're okay, I guess. But cats tend to be full of pride. Dogs, on the other hand, lick you, smell you, and bark when they need to be fed. Dogs have been part of my home for most of my life, and they have become like kids to me. I even like when they sleep with me. I love to wake to a fresh lick in the face or a bark that they are ready to get out of bed.

NEIL AND OLLIE

I treat a dog like a human. I don't mean by this that human types aren't my first love, for they are. But God made dogs to be our best friends, and the way they love is so pure and kind.

I can be real with my dogs. I am filled with such joy that God gave them to cheer us up and to love us in truth. They don't judge but are just there. They love being with me and are glad when I come home. They wait until I open the front door and then beg for treats. I give in because I am a sap for dogs.

Neil Silverberg

TRUE WORTH

The birth of my son's baby girl thrilled my heart. Julianne drew me in on day one and has held my heart ever since. The bond we've built in her first three years will last long after I am gone.

PAM WITH JULIANNE

One way that we will bond from now on is when I teach Julianne a sense of who she is as a child of God. In a world where human value is taken away prior to birth and even in the throes of death, Julianne needs to know that *God created mankind in his own image, in the image of God he created them; male and female he created them* (Gen. 1:27 NIV). Once she knows this, she will also know her true worth.

Next, I will point Julianne to God's great love for her. I will share what Jesus did on the cross to pay for her wrongs so she won't get caught in the trap of guilt and shame that shouts, "What's wrong with you?" She will learn that Jesus died to set her free and that He rose from the dead so she can be with Him now and in Heaven.

Then, I will pray that Julianne trusts in and walks with Jesus for the rest of her life so that she will not be duped by the lie of Satan: "You have no worth!" As long as she obeys the Holy Spirit, then when Satan tempts her she will be strong and choose God's best.

And for all this, at the end of my life, I will be able to close my eyes and trust that I will see Julianne again when her Heavenly Father calls her Home.

Pamela Rosales

BUSH FLIGHT

What is it like?

I speak not of big jets with rows of chairs and screens as in film shows. I think not of rooms seven seats wide where girls bring trays as in bars. I speak of a four-seat plane which I fly.

Come with me.

Let's take to the sky at will — wheel and whirl with hawks and dance with rain birds high over the ground.

FAY AND SALLY SMITH
WITH SON STEPHEN

Let's choose the sun side of a cloud to see the arch of God. Red, green, and blue shines the rain.

Let's plunge into the storm to feel its strength. So soon we pass from day to night, bounce up and down and 'round in hard drafts of wind. Rain slams against glass. As fast as we are thrust in, we break out. It's light again.

There's a call. A lad is hurt. He needs help now. Go full speed, straight line. Land. Put him in the tip-back chair. Waste no time. Take off. Doc waits at the next strip. One more life is saved.

It's time to head home. Let's fly down a stream to spot crocs, cliff birds, and dug-out boats. Let's dip our wings to friends who reach up to wave. Let's skim tops of trees to see blooms of gold, red, or white set in a mass of green — spread out like a huge green rug as far as the eye can see. Climb high above all, on top of the world's hurt and pain, hate and wounds. See the plane's lines shaped like a cross on a cloud below us. Here the world looks calm, full of peace and joy.

We must glide to land again.

How can we tell kin and friends what it's like? There's no way.

We join earth folk as if we've been on ground all day, but in our hearts we keep lots of thoughts about our time in the sky. The flight was so other-world. Yet we know it was real.

Some sweet day they'll go with us. Then they too will know bush flight in a small plane.

Fay Henry Smith

TO SLEEP

Ever since I was a child, I've loved to sleep – to scrunch down cozy under heavy quilts when the room is dark and cool. After I hit the sack, sleep comes soon.

It comes over me like the tide upon the shore. It washes the day away like a house of sand, to cleanse my soul of the cares that have built up. Sleep pulls my mind into the great deep Gulf Stream to flow for these few hours and carry me at its will, not mine.

While there, I tend to have good dreams that I enjoy. I am blessed not to have to deal with any image of the ugly, the scary, the trapped, or the fierce — at least not often. It's not that I don't have rage or loss or feel weak at times. I guess my id just copes with those in other ways. It's mercy that leaves my sleep alone. Still, the themes of the dreams do come back — again and again. Scenes change and plots change, but the same threads are there. It's how we deal with the stuff of life.

But to sleep well is not a given. On the nights when I don't, some things can help. At times, I can talk my body into being at rest, even if my mind is not. Most of the time, I can pray and find that I fall right back to sleep even when I'm not done with my prayer list. If it takes a long time, I give thanks that God is there to be with me and to hear me in the night.

To sleep is to heal my whole self.

Dottie Lovelady Rogers

23

THE SCRIBE

From His throne, His grin can be felt — each time I sit and pen the words He gives me. At what point did He say, "I think I will place in this one the gift of prose"?

But my first piece was a rhyme for my dog. She died one night — hit by a car. I was a boy, then. I may be old now, but I can still quote each line of that poem.

Years have passed. I learned the craft with pen and ink, or I'd just sit and type.

Thank God for white-out.

These days my Mac is warm with use, the keys worn off by my muse — the Lord.

What I write might be a new book or my old blog. I scroll down and up, armed with a cup of joe and the love of words. Where did I last leave off?

Then it starts, with a thought — a clue my mind plays back. Often, these are words that help me find God in that flash of time. He helps me see the bridge that joins my life path with His Word. And so, from my heart it wakes — that new world birthed from one point in time.

For me, to write this is to make God smile.

I love that.

Tez Brooks

SITTING ON THE GRANDS

L ike most dads, I loved to play and rough house with my kids. It was fun for me to make them squeal and laugh. One way was to act as if I would sit on them. I wouldn't try to put my full weight on

LEFT TO RIGHT: CAROLINE, HENRY, AVERY, TOM, KAYLEE, SHELBY (BACK), ALEXA

them, but I didn't tell *them* that. They loved it and laughed and squealed.

These days, I am glad I can sit on my six "grands" (my kids' kids). When my young grands watch TV, I walk in front of the chair where one or two sit. I turn to face the TV and act as if I'm caught up in the show. Since I block their view, they yell out, "Papa, move! We can't see!" I then step back close to them and put my hands on the arms of their chair while I look at the TV. I squat down close, but do not sit on them. They laugh and yell for me to get up. They put up their short legs and push and kick at me. I move my rear end to get past their legs to light on their laps but not to press down. I say out loud to their moms, "This chair has lots of lumps." Then I twitch some more. "We need to throw out this chair. It has loud lumps in it." My grands squeal again. When I get up, they yell out to me, "Do it one more time, Papa." I move back to the chair and "sit" down on them once more. They squeal and squirm just as they did the first time.

Any kids who then come into the room will run up to the chair and hop on it with the rest of the kids. "Now me!" I hear them shout. Of course, I have to grant their wish. It is their right as penned in the PaPa Code Book. As long as they let me do it, I will sit on my grands. To tell the truth, I love it as much as they do.

Tom Kennedy

25

My Heart Swells

When I think of Him, I smile — at all the things He's done for me and the way He's loved me. And my heart swells.

I used to run from Him, fueled by pain and guilt. I couldn't look back for fear I'd see His tears. One day I could run no more. Legs weak, breath sapped, I fell to my knees and cried out, "Lord, I need you! I have not lived the way I should. I hid in the midst of fear and shame. I can't see past my pain."

He raised my face to meet His. In it I saw a strong chin and cheeks — as pale pink as a rose, yet firm below the laugh lines. When our eyes met, I saw His love.

"Do not run or hide from me," He said. "I died on the cross for you. No more pain, no more shame."

I could taste the salt from my tears.

Who is this man with love so deep that He would die on a cross? He knew my past, yet loved me. If you were to ask me why I love the Lord, that's it. He took my place on the cross. No more shame, fears, or doubt. I am free.

No more do I have to run from my pain and shame and turn my back on the one who loves me. I am free from my past. I am loved by the one who is love.

Neither height nor depth, nor anything else in all creation, will be able to separate us from the love of God that is in Christ Jesus our Lord (Rom. 8:39 NIV).

Jeanette Duby

26

Do You Need Help?

When I reached into my purse, I felt a punch in the gut. My hotel-room key was gone.

It had been a long day, and I yearned to jump into bed. I dropped to the hall floor and searched every nook of my bag. No key. I laid my head on the wood of the door jam. My feet hurt and my head throbbed.

From where I knelt by the door, my eyes half open, I saw a pair of high heels clap down the hall. By her fast steps, I knew she didn't have time to stop. Then a pair of red flats tapped by, a woman on the way to her room. *Maybe she's as tired as I am* I thought.

I was just beginning to rouse, when — two rooms down — a lady with gray curls stepped up to her door. She craned her neck, and her eyes met mine. Her face was soft and warm, like the puffy linen locked away in my room.

"Do you need help?" she asked.

"I think I'm locked out." My reply was part laugh, part sigh.

She called the front desk for me and talked with me until the hotel staff came.

I made it into the room and kicked off my shoes. When I fell into bed, I felt the sheets warm my skin, but it was the Good Samaritan who still warmed my heart.

It hadn't taken her long to halt her plans — for me. It hadn't cost her a cent, and she didn't need any skills. She used no fancy words.

But I knew that if it were Jesus at that door, He would treat me the same way she did. Her kind heart had given me a taste of His love.

Now, I want to grasp every chance to be kind. Maybe that one in need will be a tired lady, just like me. With a smile, I'll ask, "Do you need help?"

Lauren Craft

GOD'S ROLE FOR ME

love being Aunt Joy to Anna and Patrick. I think of holding them on their first days; each was so tiny in my arms. Anna's brown eyes and Patrick's blue ones would gaze up at me. With each breath they took, my heart leaped; and I fell more in love. As I held them while they slept, I would thank God for this time.

It took a while and lots of funny tries for them to learn my name. Each title they came up with was a great sound to me. I would reply to "Chewy" or "J" with a smile.

I gasp at how time has flown. They are now twelve and eight. Each time I visit they now call out, "Aunt Joy!" and give me a

JOY, PATRICK, AND ANNA

hug. I hold them and squeeze tight. Anna may treat me to a piece with her flute or show off a new dance step. Patrick often plays ball for me with such drama and joy. Other times we will learn about parts of the world with a card game. I hear the thrill in Anna's voice as she shares a part of a story she's made up. I hear Patrick's glee as he makes his cars race on their tracks. At times they ask me to pray for them or their friends. On the days when they are sad or scared, I hurt with them and ask God to help them.

The years whiz by, and I want to hit pause. I savor each laugh and each story. I find joy in my role as an aunt, and I thank God for the job.

Joy E Miller

FICTION

(PAGES 39–61)

ONE MORE DAY

She stood at the end of the dirt road that led the way home.
Pink wild blooms grew on its sides; each one had felt the kiss of dust that the cars flung in the air as they sped by. Tall pines stood in a row like guards who keep watch for friend or foe.

Her thoughts took her to days long gone. Days of trees to climb, mud pies to mix, and swings that made her toes touch the sky.

What was that? Did her mom call out to her? "Come in child, wash up for lunch!" She set her eyes on the field that ran next to the house. She was sure she saw her dad as he cut the hay from dawn to dusk. Oh, how it had the scent of home!

How is it that the trees stay green, the blooms pink, and the dust from the road the same dull brown? How can all these things stay the same when those she loved for so many years have gone?

A wisp of grey hair fell from its place, past the laugh lines near her eyes — lines that drew a map from a full life to the wish of just one more day in this place, in those times.

One more day to hear her dad sing.

One more day to pick a pink bloom and place it in her mom's hands.

Just one more day at home.

Shelley Pierce

29

REST

The room was dark and the air heavy and warm — much too warm. Two box fans, one on each side of the room, worked with all their might to move the heavy air; but the room was too large and the cribs too many. The whirr of the fans had lulled a few lucky ones to sleep. Some called out to each other with tones to match the hum of the fans. They knew no other way to bear the long, warm hours.

On this night, rest did not come for one tiny, black-haired girl. On this, as on many other nights, she sat still and quiet in her crib. She did not cry. She *had* cried, long ago when she was first brought here; but, after a time, she learned that no one would come into this dark and scary room to soothe her, even if she cried all night. No one would come in the night to feed her, change her, and rock her back to sleep. So, she sat still and stared into the room's dark chasm as the fans drummed on and on.

If only she knew that at the break of dawn, hope would be on its way! Two, with great love in their hearts, were *on their way*! Long before this night they had learned her story, loved her from afar, and worked long and hard for months and months, just to come for her. If only she knew that soon it would be all right to cry out in the night again, then she could close her eyes now, lie down, and rest.

Suzanne D. Nichols

30
LOVE LOST

My heart was rent on a cold night; the twelfth month of the year. What can I say? I liked her, loved her. Didn't we all? I sensed us close, a bond like yin and yang. We could talk and though often tense, I felt a strange calm — with her. It's odd how blind a crush can make one. You don't see the signs she gives that tell you in some way she's not yours. You keep on, in your dream.

But the stark wake feels like death: your heart shrinks. The wound spreads from just a crack: the same shape of the grin you made when you tried to be "cool" about it. And not hurt. You don't show hurt; that's the worst. You hide away the love that has died, and you are like a bird in a cage that can sing no more — its song hushed.

You try to say what they all say, that you'll meet more; you'll see more. But first the bird has to learn a new song. And right now you can find no song, no sun, no stars. There is none but you and her, and the hurt makes three.

What a curse to dream in ways of love! The heart, so strong, yet so frail. And you wish she could see where it bleeds — not to make her hurt but to make her see how much you did. And loved. And lost. But she won't know it, as your bird is gone to a place she can't be. She can't see its chipped wing or the maimed place where its chest once stood out proud. Or its feigned flight, through winds of woe. And rains. And fog.

Those are yours to know.

Alexander Chavers

31
RESCUED BY AN ANGEL

With each step Gram took, I felt more sad and more alone; but I didn't take my eyes off her. She and I marched into my "real school" side by side. First grade meant I would be solo. I think she felt my gaze. At the door she shot me a long wink, the kind she swore was an angel call. Then she left.

I put my Crayola box in my desk and moved with the class to the Happy Rug. Mrs. Beaumont said that each of us had to tell our name and the color we liked best. The girl on my right, whose name was Abigail, said she loved pink. When I got my nod, I stood — my hands in a tight knot.

"My name is Texas Elizabeth Granger, and I like yellow." The words fell out like water freed from a dam, and I took back my seat with just as much force.

"*Texas*? What kind of name is *Texas* for a girl?" Weldon Jack Davis said in a hiss. He had his hands up the way Gram held hers when the choir sang "How Great Thou Art." He looked to each side of him, as if to gauge who else was shocked. I felt my face turn red — his favorite color.

The girl to my left stood.

"I like her name! My Pap lives in Texas!" The cold glare she cast on Weldon Jack Davis dared him to ever say one more word about my name. A giant grin took over her face, and I'd just met the one who has turned out to be my best friend for life. "My name is Angel," she said,— "and I like yellow best, too."

Nicey T. Eller

IN ANY STORM

Waves lap on the shore as a breeze slides out to sea. Calm.

Yet clouds hang near — dark. A storm brews.

At first, the rain falls only a thin film on her skin as she strolls the sand. She smiles at the cool of light drops. But soon, light drops give way to pelts that sting her face. The wind swirls strong and starts to push against her body.

Her feet pick up the pace and leave quick prints in wet sand. Fear gives chase as she flies home.

At last a door, a key, and a sigh.

She peers through glass at the rage of waves and the whip of wind. A wild scene.

But what were the words of that one who also knew wild scenes as he kept flocks of sheep?

God is our refuge and strength, an ever-present help in trouble. Therefore we will not fear, though the earth give way and the mountains fall into the heart of the sea, though its waters roar and foam and the mountains quake with their surging (Ps. 46:1-3).

The pound and roar of foam-edged waves have made their sound. But now they are quiet, though not still. In the midst of their quiet, she hears the small voice of God, saying, "Fear not. You are mine, and I am with you in any storm."

She nods…smiles.

She knew that.

She did.

But once more, it was good to hear.

In this storm or in any storm.

Beverly Varnado

33
A VISIT WITH PAUL

Years back, my faith was strong, and, I thought, pure. When a false faith tries to change the old, true faith, how can a good guy like me just watch?

I was told I could go and root out those who left our faith. I thought God would bless my work. Here's the bind, though: I soon found that my old, strong faith was dead wrong.

See, the good news that those new faith groups spread brought a change of mind about our old faith. They spoke of grace and not much about laws. I'd thought that to please God I had to stop the false faith.

Yes, I held coats and stood watch as Stephen died. I saw the mob hurl stones at him. I saw him die strong in his faith. That made me begin to doubt, and I don't like to doubt. So, I had to step up my work to stop them.

I got on a horse to head out on my plan to jail or even bring some to death. Next thing I know, a flash of light sent me to the ground. I'd been struck blind — not by the bright sun, but by God's Own Son. He spoke. To me! What He said showed me that I had been dead wrong. By the time I got up, my false faith was gone.

I was led to Ananias who laid hands on me to heal me. Ever since then, my aim is to tell of God's Son, to spend my life for Him. I've gone many miles. Some hate what I teach. I may have to die for Him, but I love Him with all my heart and do not fear death. I will spread Truth as long as I have breath. Will you?

Margery Kisby Warder

SHE DARES TO HOPE

A child wakes in the dark of night, the air cool on her face. She wants to just curl back to sleep on her mat. But her mom's soft nudge tells her it's time to go, so Violet rubs her eyes, stands, and slips on a skirt and top. Her bare feet take swift steps to the place in the hut where she left the large soiled jug. With no words, she starts down the steep path. When she hears a noise from the bush, her heart jumps, but she must go on — four long miles to the pond.

With a small cup she fills her jug. It's not cold, not clean. Leaves and twigs and bugs float by. Silt clouds the pool. Her friend — her best friend — is sick from this foul stuff they all must drink. With no choice and no cure, Violet's friend might die.

As stars fade in the pale dawn sky, she lifts her gaze. *Why, God?* The jug, soon full, now weighs her down. With one hand she holds it there on her head and starts back. The way home is just as long, now lit by gold streams of light from the east. She squints and steps with care.

Once home, she grabs her books and runs to school like a slave set free. Violet breathes hard and takes her seat, keen to learn. She dares to hope she might one day treat the sick, make them well, help them live. *Lord Jesus, I trust in you. Bless us with a well. Give me a life that is full.*

Sherree Funk

PETE BITES THE DUST

I heard the thump and saw the color of rust fly in front of a car and smack the ground.

Oh no! That was a robin! I got to my feet to peer out the blinds. The bird lay still.

Was it hurt? Or worse, dead? I named it Pete.

Jeans and a shirt were close, so I put them on over my pjs. Then I found a thin board. It would serve as a scoop to bring Pete back to the house.

By now, tears ran down my face. Poor bird. I hope he's not in pain.

It didn't look as if Pete had been hit again. He also didn't move or chirp. I moved close to the bird. I think he's dead. More tears.

I bent down to slide Pete onto my board. Where was the rest of his body?

Then I knew the truth.

Pete wasn't a robin. Pete was a clump of Tennessee red clay that was under the car.

Red clay! Did I truly cry over a clump of red clay?

My grief was raw. The pain had been real. Now, I felt silly.

Pete, the clump, got a swift kick and flew to the other side of the road.

Back in the house, I wiped my eyes, blew my nose, and made a cup of tea. I got a pen and paper, sat down, and began to write Pete's obit.

Barbara D'Antoni Diggs

THREE WAYS TO SERVE

Three friends stood side by side as they had done all their lives. In the past, what one did, all would do. They were as close as strands of twine. Their lives were coiled like a piece of cord, which made them a strong team. But now, change was here.

One of them had signed up to serve his land. Months of hard work were in front of him, with boot camp first on the list. He knew it would all be worth it. Now he would be the one to watch out for those he cared for. But in truth, he did not know all that it might cost.

One of the friends chose more school. He was not sure where he would end up. He might want to teach or heal or learn a trade. There were lots of roads he could take. He would learn how to be the best he could be in his field of choice.

The third friend was bound to his home by the needs of those who were close to him. His mom and dad would count on his strength to help out in a time of great stress. For now, he chose to put them in front of his wants. They loved him more than they could say for his great heart to give up these years for them.

Once boys who played as knights, they were now men and loyal to the core. No war, no trade, no cause could break the bond they shared. That bond was fixed in their hearts, as firm and fast as the sword of lore that had been set in stone.

Liz Kimmel

I Slip, I Slide, I Got No Stride

Hey, that tiny dude down there looks like he's doing his best to split in two. "How you doing, Pal?"

"I'm lost. How you think I'm doin'? Wait a sec. Got it done. We're both lost, but at least I've got one more of me to hang with."

"You're an amoeba."

"Wow. You think so?"

"You're under my scope on high power."

"All right, Mr. Know It All, how do I get outta here?"

"Can't you see it?"

"Hello? No eyes, and no sense of, uh, you know that sense that tells you which way to go? Wish I knew how to use big words."

"Yup."

"Wanna keep going, but I bang into stuff."

"Bits of wood pulp. That's all it is, what's left of an old front page."

"A real paper trail then. And it looks easy to you? I'm about ready to hang it up."

"Don't do it."

"What? That's all you got for me?"

"You've got to trust me. If you'll just walk—"

"Hey, Buster, you don't get what's goin' on down here. You see any hands or feet on me?"

"No."

"'didn't think so. I slip. I slide. I got no stride."

"But the path is straight."

"Oh, yeh? You got a two-foot blade handy? I could use one to slash through this mess."

"But you admit you've got no hands. You couldn't swing it."

"One point for you. Get me outta here then."

"It's this way."

In all your ways acknowledge Him and He will make your paths straight.

Proverbs 3:6. NASB

David Buster

THE ROAD TO ROOTS

Not all roads that lead to the church are paved. Some, like this one, are more like wide paths of packed red clay and swirls of dirt. A shell of a house here and there fights to stand straight. In a strange way the junk cars and toys caked with grime — plus every so often a worn-out dryer — that graze in the wild yards remind him of scrap back in the city that Liza calls "art."

A whip of hot muggy wind blasts through the car as it turns onto a black tar road. *Welcome to the Deep South,* Andy thinks. He soon sees the stones with last names like his that he first saw eight years ago when his dad's mom was let go from her agony. A sense of kin tries to coax his heart. And down the street is the place he hopes will help give life to what he fears is dead: the church his dad's dad began. *Take it or leave it, these are my roots.* Andy's mind gnaws on the thought.

Once Andy's back, Liza tries to press him. "Did you find the church?" No response. With a flick of her bangs to one side, she stands her frail frame smack in front of Andy.

He rubs his thick hand over a new buzz cut. "What?" he barks back. Liza sighs. Andy turns away.

"Did it help you heal?"

"Heal?"

Liza sighs again.

"I don't know if *heal* is the right word. Let's put it this way — as Tolkien wrote, 'Not all those who wander are lost.'"

"How noble."

Andy breathes in. "I found what good was there to find…and left the rest."

Kenneth Avon White

THE SWORD OF TRUTH

Fog whisked through the open door in the cracked stone wall.

As Mia stepped into the vast, dim hall, she strained her eyes to see a gold-edged Bible on a stand. To one side, fog surged from a domed nook, where a cloaked guard stood at the head of a stone table flanked by two posts. He gripped a gold sword with the blade held flat to his chest.

Mia stared at him. "Who are you?"

The guard tapped the flat side of the sword blade to his hood, thrust it in an arc, and laid it on the table. He stepped back. Palm up, the guard's hand passed over the sword. "I guard the sword of truth."

"Can I look at it?" Mia edged into the nook until her body pushed into the cold stone. She bent close. Gems flashed and pulsed in the etched hilt of the sword.

"What is this green one?" Mia stroked it.

"Grace."

"I sure need that. What about the blue?"

"Faith in Jesus Christ."

When Mia poked a ruby, red stained her flesh, "Blood! Jesus' blood?"

"He bought you with His blood."

Mia mused, "I believe that Jesus is the way, the truth, and the life."

The guard bowed. "He grants me the power to give the sword of truth to all those who believe and will live by it."

Mia gasped, "I do believe in Him, but no one knows."

"Take it. Wield the sword with skill and fight lies with it."

Mia clutched the sword and left the nook. Fog whirled over her path, but the sword lit her way.

E. V. Sparrow

40

BREATH OF LIFE

Fire Team Three is trapped in the house," the fire chief says, "It's up to you and Jen to find them. Bring them out quick." His eyes are full of hope. "Air up."

The house is charred black and cloaked in ash. My friends, Jeff and Mike, are in a bind, lost in ruin. The hose they used snakes from the fire truck and through the door. Gray smoke, soft and thick, seeps out. My eyes sting, but not from smoke. Jen checks my air mask, and I check hers. We kneel by the wide mouth of death. I try to take slow breaths. *Jesus, please be with us. Be with them.*

We crawl through the door. I track the hose Jeff used. He's a good man. An old friend. Our church loves him. Where is he? I can't see through the dark smoke, so I close my eyes. We work through the wreck on our hands and knees. We have to find them! Where is he? Time drags. I find a boot. I crawl to him. He's stuck. He grabs my arm. But I hear Jen yell for help. I reach for her. Nothing. She yells once more.

"Go," he gasps. "She needs you. She needs Jesus." He smiles. My heart aches. But I know he's right.

I leave my friend.

Where is Jen? *God, help!* Screams. Sweat bites my eyes. I hear the air-pack bell. She's low on air. Where is she? I find a boot. Her boot. I feel a tug at my arm, and I pull.

Out of the house now. Jeff is gone. Jen has burns, but breathes clean air. "You came back for me," she sobs. "You saved me."

I smile. "No, Jesus saved us both. Jeff told me tell you His story."

Bob Adauto

41

BEING SURE

She sat in her dark blue lift chair. Head back. Eyes shut. Thoughts ran through her mind. Scenes of days past. The man of her dreams…gone…long ago. Many years she'd lived here with him and their brood of four — two boys and two girls. Those were fun times of young growth, school, more kids-in-law, and then empty nest again with only the two of them. Years of joy and love, not lack. Hard work and play.

She felt okay with her life. She'd done the best she could. But, life was change. She'd said "yes" with her eyes wide open. They were open now. She ran them over the room, bare of photos and knick-knacks taken and bought on trips to other states and the rest of the world. This was the last day she'd spend in her home.

She gazed out to her front yard. Where the glass panes let the sun come in bright beams to the edge of her chair, she saw the For-Sale sign. Change was ahead — the one she'd fought for years — the next place to live, this time with old ones like her. She couldn't gripe. Her kids had been there when she was in want or bad health.

Still, change wasn't easy. She shut her eyes, a tear slid down her lined cheek, then one more.

The ring of her cell-phone woke her. "Mom, I can't do this. I've been on the phone with my sibs. You'll move in with me. I'll take care of you, now. Bill's okay with this. The kids can't wait. Will you come and live with us?"

"Yes!" she said, her heart in her throat. "Are you sure?"

"Yes, Mom. We're sure."

Reba Rhyne

42

Hope on the Wing

I don't know what to do, Lord. We could lose our home." Sarah
cries. She kneels by the bed — where she has slept alone ever
since her Samuel died in the mine. Sarah holds up the bills to the
only Hope she has.

"I try to be a good mom — to love my kids and teach them about
You and Your love. How you left the ninety-nine to come for the one
who was lost. Please, Lord, our home needs that kind of love again."

Sarah lays the debts on the quilt her mom made for her and Samuel.
Soon the kids will wake. She dries her tears.

I will not think of lack today but take joy in what I have.

"Rise and shine, my dears. This is the Lord's Day. We'll be going
down the mount soon."

After eggs and bacon, with their Sunday best on, they start the walk
to the flat land.

Jacob holds Emma's hand. Sarah holds Lorelie on her back since
Lorelie is too young for the big-rock paths ahead.

Jacob looks up above the tree line. "Hey, Mama, there goes a hawk.
Look at the size of those wings! 'bet he could fly to the top of Mt.
Nebo."

Sarah looks up. "I'm sure you're right, son." She smiles. "It makes
my heart right glad to see birds take flight like that."

"I want to fly like that big bird, Mama," Emma sighs.

As the hawk flies next to the sun, Sarah starts her song. "Jesus loves
me; this I know —"

"This is the day the Lord hath made. We will rejoice and be glad
in it," Jacob adds.

Sarah turns, fixes Jacob's cap and puts Emma's stray hair in place.
"Yes, my loves. We'll fly again. You'll see. We'll fly again."

Mary Lester

43

EMPATHY

"How rude! That kid wouldn't work for me. Not for long, that is."

"It's not his fault, George. He's not the one in charge. Calm down."

"But he's the one who lost our bags and made me miss the game."

"So, you think he should lose his job?" Wanda asked. "Why not can his boss? Would you stand still while your boss yelled at you that way? Who made the rules? I feel for the guy. You had a boss like that once, and what did you do? You walked out. Let's just take a seat, like he said. I need to get off my feet."

George stood where he could watch as new bags dropped. Round and round. Black bags, brown bags, large bags, small bags. Bags from Miami but not one from Chicago. Most of them gone with just one pass.

Wanda kept her eyes on George. When the red from his neck reached his face, he would need two of his pills. They were for his Type A, but George told folks they were for his heart.

She watched as he pulled his phone from his belt. "*Who could that be? The kids should be at work by now.*"

"Dad, you left your bags by the front door," their daughter said. "Didn't you think about them when you checked in? What do you want me to do?"

"Ship them. I'll send you the cash."

Wanda joined George at the desk — just in time to hear him say, "We found our bags. By the way, I once had a boss like yours. It's tough."

As we walked away, George looked back to smile, nod, and wave.

"Wanda, where are my car keys?"

"In one of the bags."

Rita Klundt

44

TO HONOR HER HERO

The sun beams down on 77 acres of broad green lawns. The old woman gulps at the view of the sad site at the edge of Nettuno, Italy — a place of death, yet so full of color and life. Roman pines line up to form an army of trees. Rows of white spots with no end dot the grass; there are 7,861 of them. *Will I ever find the right one?* she thinks.

She holds tight to a slip of paper that is meant to be her guide. "What will I say to him?" she says to the woman by her side but not to ask her. "It's been so long; I want to say the right thing." And then — there it is. The spot bears a last name that is the same as hers. Tears well up in her eyes. She feels love and pride for this man even though she hasn't seen him since 1944. And she won't see him now. All that is before her is a cross with his vital info —- name, date of birth, and date of death. He died in World War II. He gave his all — for the U.S., for *her.*

"Hi, Joe," she says in a soft voice. "It's me. I know you've been gone for years, but you are still alive in my heart," she says with a deep sigh. "You're a hero to me, and you'll be a hero even after I am gone." With a proud look at the young woman next to her, she adds, "I told our girl here about you so she can write your story for many to read. You are her hero, too."

After a bit, the women turn to leave. This visit to their hero's grave must end, but their honor for him never will.

Alice H. Murray

45
FEAR AND PEACE HAVE A CHAT

One day, Fear and Peace sat down to chat. Each one felt they had the most strength. Fear tried to stare down Peace, while Peace eyed Fear with a look of deep calm.

Then the fight was on!

Fear went first. "I give a man a dream of doom," he said "that will replay in his head until he goes out of his mind."

Peace said, "I bring calm to all who seek me."

Then Fear began to brag of those who fear snakes, heights, and death — to name a few. Peace thought a bit, and in a soft quiet tone began to list her best: "the heart at rest, the mind that stills, and the breath that breathes slow and even."

Fear boomed, "I bring fear of loss and being sick!"

Peace said, "I am the calm in the storm and hope after loss."

Fear got mad and began to yell that he makes men think they will fail or die poor. Peace, in a soft voice, said that she likes to tell men that to fail is not the end and that soon they can soar above their loss.

She said, "The poor learn to be rich in ways not bought or sold."

Fear took out a large glass ball and thrust it in Peace's face. He wagged his finger with a smirk. Caught in the ball was a man in a panic who shook over and over again. "Beat that," he said.

When Peace took the glass ball, a young boy came to the man and put his arm on him and he shook no more. "Peace wins," she said with a smile. "Fear may start it, but Peace will end it!"

Sharon Atwood

46

MYRTLE

The spring eve sky still holds its blue tint as Myrtle leaves work. It has been a hot, hard day using the hefty iron on sheets and towels. She does not have the five cents for the cable car so she begins the walk up the hill to her house a mile away. Her feet have been in the well-worn, hardy black pumps since 7 A.M., and they cry out with each step. She thinks of the meat, spuds, and green beans she will cook for her spouse and her brood of five. She is glad for the bread and pies she baked on Saturday.

In the quiet at the top of the hill, Myrtle looks down at the sight she knows so well. Mid-river are Willamette Falls' swirls of white water that plunge over rocky crags down to the calm river's floor. Her heart tells her that God, who made the falls, has been with her all her life. He was there when they moved from Oklahoma, one babe still in arms, to Oregon City. He is there when her two small girls tease each other and her older ones talk of being off in the world very soon. God is there when her spouse pulls pranks, and all laugh till their sides ache. He is with her now, tired body and sore feet.

She vows to keep God's peace close in all she does when she turns to walk to the place with the sights, sounds, and scents that are part of who she is — to the place that is home for all she loves most.

Pamela Groupe Groves

SALVATION CHURCH

He wears black pants, the type you see at a store that sells clothes for less than a can of soup. His short blonde hair shines with gel, and the chain that hangs from his belt sweeps as he sways. I keep my steps quiet. I don't want to make loud, in this place.

I feel a sense of warmth in this place of few — not even 12 of us — many fewer than the home church where I first sat this day. When I got there; the sun was new, the noise of music loud, with many a voice to join in. But, now, here, is when I awake.

On his ear, a jewel hangs low. On an arm is the blue, red, green, black of an image I do not know.

I do know the song he sings. I sing now, too — in this place where a dime is gold. My shoes may cost dimes more, but we are the same.

My eyes drift down. I bow. I sense a holy light of wind and fire. It has been a long time. Here is holy flame — where ones come from a hovel, a shed, a shack of no dimes, of lost minds, of drugs, of ills.

My eyes lift to see the one with the chain that drags low on a leg of black cloth as he moves. His feet take him out of the pew and move him up to the cross. He kneels. He lays his gelled blonde head on a stair.

Rest.

I sway, and the holy, light wind blows in this place where a dime is gold.

Lynn J. Simpson

20 Hands High

The rain stood so thick that was as if God had sent yet one more flood to rid the world of man. The earth below — drowned for days — could hold no more. The river had reached its crest. The levee would soon break. Every man, woman, and child in Tic Hollow had fled. All but Tom, for he could not go. Grans' heart beat was slow; her skin pale, and Death sat on a stool near the old black Singer sewing machine as if it had not a thing to do but wait.

Tom's kin had told him to leave Grans. They said that Grans would greet him in the sweet by and by. But Tom, made of a gnarl of root that doesn't give way in a storm, did not fear death. His only fear was God, for that was all he need fear.

As the river began to creep up on the cabin floor, Grans set her eyes on Tom. He, in turn, moved her hand up to his heart as he bent to hear her frail voice.

"He is here," Grans said.

"Who is here, Grans?" Tom asked, aware that Death still sat upon the stool.

"Jesus," she replied.

Tom's great frame began to shake as he saw that the stool was now empty.

"Tom…He…He has made a way," Grans said with her last breath.

Tom, the water to his knees, took Grans into his arms. He would greet the river as it rose more and more — on his own terms. But then he saw what should not have been. There by the porch stood the lost mule, Moses, 20 hands high, with a bit in his mouth. The enemy of Death had made a way.

Paul A. Hinton

49

HIS WAY

No!" Amanda said and grabbed her purse. "Some blind dates may work, but they're not for me. I think if God's plan is for me to meet a man, He'll do it His way in His time. You don't just fall in love. You *fall* into ditches."

"Okay. We get it. No blind dates for you," Chloe said. In her mind, she crossed off her list that great guy from church — the one who fights fires.

Amanda clipped a leash on her dog. "I may not have a date, but Trixie does — with her vet. 'later!'"

She saw the taxi but too late. It ran the light and hit her jeep so hard that it flipped over. Amanda blacked out. As help came, Trixie jumped from the car and ran.

The next day, with two black eyes and a head still sore, Amanda was lying on her couch when a knock at the door made her jump. On her porch stood a man she thought she'd seen at church from afar. The sight of what squirmed in his arms made her tear up: a happy ball of fur with a collar that read *Trixie*.

"I've been hunting for you," he said. "When we were called to the scene, the first thing I saw was this scamp at a full sprint away from your car. She led me on a merry chase then, but I'm glad where she's led me today!"

Amanda smiled. "Come in,'" she said as she reached for Trixie. "Do you like iced tea?"

Penny L. Hunt

TO HOLD THEIR HANDS

Grief fills Jane's chest as the third of her kin is laid to rest in the space of a year. Head in her hands, she reels.

"What'll I do now? My life's tied to the care of those who're now gone."

She's been told, to care is joy. But it doesn't feel true.

"If this is my gift Lord, to love the sick 'til they die, then I don't want it! It hurts too much!"

An old soul sits down on the pew next to Jane. Eyes bright, the aged one sighs "I won't tell you your loss is for the best, as some do. But take heart. All who've had air fill their lungs have known loss. Our Christ felt grief."

Jane sniffs, "He did?"

"Christ said, *'My heart is crushed with grief to the point of death.'* He cried, *'My Father...let this cup of suffering be taken away from me.'** There is no ache our Lord has not known. God knows pain. To hold the hands of the ill as they take their last breaths, what gift could give more joy? Ease fear? Bring peace?"

Tears fall down Jane's cheeks at the truth of what the old one says. She feels a warm, frail hand slip into hers. "Can we know joy, Jane, if we've not known woe?"

Jane bows her head, "Thank you Lord, for my pain, and for my gift. May it be a source of peace for those I love. Christ's grief on the cross brings the joy of life to us all. May I not lose sight of You in the hurt of my heart."

*Matthew 26:38-39 NLT

Leah Hinton

NON-FICTION
RESUMES

ABOVE ALL ELSE

Not long ago I was asked what things I prized most. I was stumped. Other than loved ones, what did I prize more than the rest? As I thought about this, a true tale from my past came back to make it plain.

Years ago we lived on the farm where my spouse grew up. The old home we moved into had been the one in which he lived all his youth. The land in this neck of the woods had not been farmed in any way. It was raw land, and we used it as ranch land for our mares. In some areas, the grass was left to grow tall. Hot arid days of wind parched the grass to make it ideal for fire. We were on guard at all times — on days like this.

And the day came. We heard that a fire burned five miles away. It could not be curbed and would reach us in less than half an hour. I was urged to pack what I could in case the fire began to lick at our heels.

In no time I had packed the car with a few things for our three girls, who were at school; my man, who was at work; and me. When I stopped to catch my breath, I was stunned to see that the items I had packed for me were my Bible that God wrote and the words that I wrote.

That day, the wind changed and our place was saved. But the event serves as proof of what I prize above all else.

Joylene M. Bailey

52

EACH NEW DAWN

The pond lies quiet and still as the sun brings forth a new dawn. Misty gray turns to soft blue. Wisps of pink…hints of orange… streaks of rose, each color the sky. All too soon the pale hues give way to the sun's bright rays; gone until they come back at dusk.

Birds wake and sing their praise to the One who gives the song. I add my songs of praise to theirs. How could I not?

SANDY'S VIEW OF THE SUNRISE OVER THE POND

Puffy white clouds float through the morn on wind I feel but do not see. The clouds shift from the shape of a dog, to a horse, and even a child as they march by.

The grass is moist under my bare feet. I smile and bury my toes into the blades as chill bumps run up my legs. The ripe berry calls my name. I reach down, pluck it from the vine, and pop it into my mouth. I close my eyes, then pray.

Lord, I adore You and thank You for this day and all it holds. I praise your holy name. You are the Maker of all good things. Above the earth. In the earth. And under the earth. You bring joy. You bring hope. You bring peace with each new dawn.

And so I begin my day. Ready for what He might place in my path.

Sandy Kirby Quandt

53
KIDS WITH NO HOMES

Often I will walk through Old Strathcona, a nice area where I like to shop. When I am done, I get in my car or hop on the bus to go home.

But what if I could not go home? What if I did not have a home to go to?

I see many teens in this area who are on their own. Kids with no homes — lost youth, not yet sure of who they are, with no one to guide them or to love them. They sleep on the street; they play music and sing for food or eat the bits they can find. How can a child make any kind of way in life if it is hard to just live day to day? It hurts my heart.

Can we help these kids who fall through the cracks? Sure, we have a part to play. We can be kind when we pass them on the street, while we enjoy the space in which we play and in which they must live. We can reach out to them and give them hope. Maybe this means that we will give money to those who give these kids a place to stay. Some of us might even choose to open our own homes to them.

"The King will reply, 'Truly I tell you, whatever you did for one of the least of these brothers and sisters of mine, you did for me'" (Matt. 25:40 NIV). Let us think of Jesus' words when we meet these young ones, too.

Katherine Kavanagh Hoffman

54
To Sleep — All Night

In my book, a good night's rest beats a hot cup of joe. Oh, I like my cup after the sun comes up as much as any other or more so. But, at my age I must drink it lead-free or so says my doc. Not-good sleep and not-good joe make for a not-good day.

If I don't get that good night's sleep, I must work in a nap by noon or a rest-my-eyes break late in the day.

Most of my naps are short. A cat nap is a good way to think of them. In these naps, I still hear sounds in the room. At any time, I can sit up and have no fog in my brain in a snap. What I need in this type of nap is just to let my thoughts drift for a while. I have to rest my eyes and let the tears wet them. Then I can go back to my tasks and not have my eyes burn and roll back in my head. I can think once more. I can get things done.

But I could have been spared all of that nap stuff if I could have had a good night's rest. Once in a while I do get blessed with a good sleep — for six whole hours. I love those nights, but they are too few.

At times, so are the naps.

Charles J. Huff

55

STAND UP FOR JESUS!

In my youth I liked to sing the hymn, "Stand Up for Jesus" in church. But at times I have thought, *Would I have the strength to stand up for Him in front of my peers?* Since I am not one who likes to stand out, I could only hope that I would.

Then God gave me a chance to find out.

As a mom of teens, I sat in a large hall filled with high school grads and their fans. We had come to hear these teens share their skills in music as they sang and played. Since this was not a Christian school, my heart beat with joy when one girl said she would sing her song "for my Lord." Her face glowed as she sang words that praised God. Though I didn't know her, I burst with pride that she would stand for Christ and share her faith.

After she ended her song, I jumped up and clapped for her. I stood alone — but I did not care.

One mom near me said, "She was good, but not *that* good." This mom had often told me she was *not* a Christian and did *not* want to be one.

I smiled at her and said, "Since she stands up for my Lord, I want to stand up for her."

This was only a small test. But I felt pleased that God gave me the strength to stand up for Jesus and honor the Lord. It helped me to know that Jesus is more than a song on my lips. He is alive in my heart.

Lydia E. Harris

I CAN'T WRITE

Jill cried . . .
I thought I could write!
I can't write.
It wasn't said; it's what I heard.
The child of my heart — my gift to God — is all marked up.
It hurts.
A lot.
I can't write.
It wasn't said; it's what I heard.
What now?
Do I throw it out?
Is it that bad?
What now, God?

God spoke . . .
You can't write?
It wasn't said; it's what you heard.
You are the child of My heart, but now you're hurt.
You can't write?
It wasn't said; it's what you heard.
Don't throw it out.
You can write.
You write from the heart.
You write for Me.
You can write.
I love your gift.
I love you, Jill.

Jill Maisch

THIS MAN, MY SON

I watch this man, my son, flip food on the grill. He is proud of these gifts he cooks. His friends stand 'round, beers and smokes in hand. His hug is real when he greets me. But I don't know him on days like this.

I want him to stay by my side so we can talk, be who we used to be. But the friends call, the ones he thinks are true. All they have done is lead him down the wrong path, and he has gone.

When he was young, I knew his heart. We made cards, baked, then took these works of love to Grandma. We hiked in the park by the pond and fed bread to the ducks. We talked of how God made all we saw and that it was good. He told me how he chose the boy at school who had no friends to be his best bud. I think of the day he cried when the boys on the back street didn't want to hear about the Jesus he loved.

And bit by bit they wore him down. He craved their praise more than our love. And as soon as he could, he left our home to find his own way, their way.

I still reach out to him with my love. At times, he comes, and I see that the boy I know is not like them. I pray that one day, he will go back to his true self, the one made by God.

Lord, I know you can draw his heart back to you — and me.

Susan Reith Swan

A NEW SENSE

With His twelve — among the 5,000 who were there to hear Him but who also longed for that other kind of food — Jesus said, *"Give them you to eat"* (Mark 6:37). This, the order of His words in the Greek, gives us a new sense of what these words could mean.

Give: with open hands and heart, with joy for what the gift will do. In them. In you.

Them: those who are in need of food — those who are lost, those in pain, those who are sad, those who weep, those drowned in guilt, those who do not know that what they long for is the one true God whom they have not yet found.

You: a mom who cares for her kids; a dad whose job keeps him busy; a pupil who learns with drive; one who is old in the world and wise; one who has much to give. You. Me. All of us.

To eat: to take in so that one can be full, to be whole in Christ, to live in Him alone

With this order of words, we can find a new way to see what Jesus said. Here He told the twelve — and tells us, as well — "Give them your life, the new life God chose to open to you, the life of love and mercy, the life of grace and peace. Show them that light so full in you that it spills over, upon, and into them. Give them your art, your music, your work, with hands and heart and will for only this — to give, to pour out, for God's glory."

For you — we — are Jesus to them.

Jesus tells us, "Give them you to eat."

Marcia Lee Laycock

AN OVERFLOWING URN

May the God of hope fill you with all joy and peace as you trust in him,
so that you may overflow with hope by the power of the Holy Spirit.

Romans 15:13 NIV

When I chose to fill my urn, I took some tips from the pros. They said, "You need a shoot to thrill, a plant to fill, and a vine to spill." To thrill, I used a Cana lily, which will grow tall and bloom a bright red — sure to catch the eye. I then added a plant that would fill the empty space and a vine that would spill over the side.

When I was done, I stood back and took a look. I was happy with what I saw. It made me think of Jesus and what He does in our lives.

When we first hear the Good News, the seed of the Gospel is being sown. When it all makes sense to us and we pledge our lives to Jesus, that is a thrill — hyper joy such that we have never known before. Jesus fills that empty space. He hides the dirt and gives us peace. We trust Him as Lord and look to Him to guide us. We obey and serve, and He fills our lives even more. He gives us so many good gifts that we can't hold back His joy. It spills out of our lives like the vine out of the pot. We must share His gifts; we must share this hope.

And so the seed will be sown again, and many a branch from the true vine will fill the land. As Jesus said, *"I am the vine; you are the branches. If you remain in me and I in you, you will bear much fruit; apart from me you can do nothing"* (John 15:5 NIV). May we all bloom and bear fruit in Him.

DESIREE'S FLOWERING URN

Desiree Glass

DEEP DOWN FAITH

M y momma and daddy are gone now. Yet the faith and the farm they left me and mine are like a vault full of gold.

While the faith can't be seen with the eyes in my head, it's as real as the dirt in the field on the farm. It is as real as the seeds that are sown. It is as real as the crops that are grown. It's as deep as the pond on the farm that schools the fish that eat the worm on the hook of my cane pole.

BECKY WITH A PHOTO
OF HER PARENTS

Her name was Rose. Her heart was as sweet and pure as her name. She taught me to love soul-deep, to pray at all times, and to bake a moist pound cake. Rose couldn't carry a tune of music, but she did carry God's word in her heart. She hid it there. Twice she had to bury a son of her own, and she did so with great strength and grace.

His name was John, the same name as the one Jesus loved. Daddy had a wit as dry as the farm in dire need of rain. John used to say that any day he got to wet a worm made for a fine day. With bait and boat, he would fish from sun up to sun down just in case the next sun to rise made for a day not so fine.

Rose and John are with God — which is right and good, for they are His. And I am His and theirs and I feel so rich.

Becky Hitchcock

ART AND SOUL

In front of the van Gogh, I sat — with tears in my eyes. The piece, "Wheatfield with Crows," spoke into my life and touched the truth in my pain: Joy and agony can exist as one in the same space, side by side, over and under and through. The two can weave in and out of a life, a mind, a heart, and also one's art — as was the case with Van Gogh.

In the strokes of his brush, I saw his inner push and pull of mania highs and grief lows. My eyes could feast on happy strokes in bright shades of sun as it shone down on gold wheat fields, full of life; happy strokes of rich olive grass and a royal blue sky with patched, linen clouds. But my heart reached out to sad strokes as the sky blurs to ink and black crows swarm, out of the dark, down and out at me.

Oh, Van Gogh! Your art — that mix of calm and storm — speaks still. It hits my heart, my home, my life. But I know that through locked bar and racked mind, you saw grace in the world. Each stroke of paint freed your soul, gave life and love for the world to see. And it calls to me. It tells me that God can and does offer hope — and light — in the dark. He takes our pain and turns it into joy. The pain does not end. It just makes the art of our lives more — so much more.

Connie Inglis

Note: View the van Gogh image here: https://www.vangoghmuseum.nl/en/collection/s0149V1962

62

IN THAT WAY

The pain burned like harsh lye in my veins, all the time. It stung as if barbed wire were wrapped round my legs all the time. The pain seared my nerves as if my legs were held to flame, all the time. The pain used up my words, my brain, my tears, and my sense of self, all the time.

Some can stay there — live at the end of their rope, scared they will not die. I chose to fight, to climb. Since I can't be who I was, I must be who I am. Look out not in. Find in me some light to share in a world of gloom. A world filled with fear and hurt and pain.

When I made the choice to live past the pain, I found hope and peace and joy, but in time, not all at once. God knew I had few ways to cope — and no way to bounce back on my own. He put those in my life who could care for me, pray for me, and teach me.

When I made the choice to make peace with my fears, with my pain, I could set to one side those things that bound me. I could learn to close my eyes and turn to those who hurt, too. I could share what I learned. In that way, I am healed.

Jorja Davis

63

Kisses for Him

Being full of the Holy Spirit, [Stephen] gazed intently into heaven and saw the glory of God, and Jesus standing at the right hand of God.

Acts 7:55 NASB

One day as I read the part of the Bible when Stephen was being stoned to death, one part burned in my mind, that he saw Jesus as He stood at the right hand of God. I knew why Jesus would stand up for Stephen since he died for the cause of Christ. This led me to think. *Would Jesus stand up for me?* At that time, I didn't think so. My life was not like Stephen's. This made me sad.

JUDY WITH HER KIDS: MISTY, DUSTY, CHRISTIAN

Later, I began to learn that God doesn't call each one of us to show our love for Him in the same way. We may all read our Bible, pray, and learn a Bible verse. But some like to sing or dance or shout! Others like to sit quiet or raise their hands in praise. As for me, I love to pray and sing as I walk or run.

One day while I ran, I gazed up at the sky and blew God a great big kiss — the first of many. After one such kiss, I fell down and cut my knee. My kids saw my wound and said, with a look of fear on their faces, "O Mom, please don't tell a soul that you blew God a kiss." My son once told me, "Mom, you're weird;" but I say, "God wants our praise. He loves us just as we are and just the way we show that praise."

My kids are grown now, but oh the joy to walk in their house and see a Bible verse taped to the wall or hear one of them ask, "Mom will you pray for me?"

Would Jesus stand up for me? I'm not sure, but one night God sent me a dream that turned my gloom into joy. In it, I went to Heaven and when Jesus saw me, He took my face in His hands and said, "Judy, do you know how many times you've blown Me a kiss?"

Judy Webster Powers

64
THE SIEVE

When a girl's life is fixed on things that can break — a name, clear skin, man's praise, or wide fame — then fear is the only sieve she can rely on to catch what is worth her heart and to lose what isn't. I used to care for a lot of things; right things. Not long ago, I wrote about them for many to read. The next day, I fell ill. All things right took a left. I trashed my first draft and out with it went those cares. Those "right" things.

I care for fewer things, now, and they are true things, whole and real things — the ones that can make it through a new sieve. True worth is a fine catch. Love, a gem as well, will not slip through life's cracks. And Christ — oh, He leads us down His own path. It is whole and real — just right for this new draft of my life.

When we breathe our last and take leave of this world, we also leave in our wake what those who stay think about us, the way they sum up who we were. I once cared to leave a great mark on the world; a noble tale to be told of me, a grand gift to those left here on earth. And though I still do, the care is not as strong. I do not ache for this grand tale as much as to live my tale in full. With those I love. With Christ who stands. If I have these few things and God's Word, I can hold fast when death taunts. This is my care now; this true thing, the Sieve of God.

Kelly Carlson

A New Call

Each day my blog feed checks a few web sites with thoughts for the day. One day I read, *Blessed are those who are persecuted because of righteousness, for theirs is the kingdom of heaven* (Matt. 5:10-12 NIV).

The same week, a friend at church gave me an issue of *The Voice of the Martyrs*. "You should read this," she said. I took it home and tossed it on a pile of mail.

The next week, my mom showed me an issue of *Decision* by The Billy Graham Evangelistic Association. It told the plight of a bake shop that might be forced to close since the owner wouldn't make a cake for two gay men who planned to marry.

I thought, *'time to obey God's nudge.*

I read my mom's *Decision* and my friend's *The Voice of the Martyrs*. Both told story after story about those who bear the name of Christ and those who aim to harm them.

The face of one young Middle Eastern mom caught my gaze. Her sad, brown eyes stared back at me. The thin child in her arms looked about two years old. I read her tale and cried.

She had met her spouse in a home church. He was a godly man who shared God's Word with the group. They fell in love. Less than five years later, he was killed. A hate crime, aimed at those who claim Christ as Lord, stole away the life they had with each other. Their story pierced my heart.

I felt a new call: to learn more about those who stand up for their faith, spread the news of their plight, and pray for them.

Jeanetta R. Chrystie

66

WHEN FAITH DOESN'T MOVE MY PAIN

Months after a car wreck, I sit at my desk with my work spread in front of me. Pin pricks of pain poke my head and jab my face. My eyes blur and my head aches. It hurts to think.

I have faith. But God didn't heal me.

Tears drip down my cheeks. I didn't get my way, but my next steps pull me out of my funk.

Six Things I Do When My Way and God's Way Don't Agree:

- **Think about what I can do, not what I can't.** On days when I can't think, I use my hands. When I can't read, I go for a walk. When I can't work, I groom my dogs.
- **Go back to basics.** God is not mean. When my life is a mess, I can trust His heart. God has a plan to use hard times for good.
- **Feel.** I stomp my feet, pound my desk, and cry while I talk to God and spill out all my woes.
- **Reach out.** I call and ask a friend to pray for me. I talk about my pain. I don't hold it in.
- **Change my focus.** I work my way out of the slump with kind acts. I send a carßßd to lift the spirit of a friend or bake a cake to share.
- **Thank God for what I have.** I list small things like the sun on my face, my pets, or my spouse who loves me in spite of my flaws. When I think good thoughts, I feel joy begin in me.

You are good and do only good; teach me your decrees.
Psalm 119:68 NLT

Shauna Hoey

TO KNOW GOD

Why should I know God? He is the one who made all things that are. Since He made me in His image, then to know Him is to know who I am. He made me to be my true self and to do any task He needs of me. To know God is to take my right place in His world.

God in Jesus is the Christ, the one who bore my sins on the cross. Through His cross, He gives me a chance to live a full life. To know Him is to be saved from death of body and soul. God is the one who helps me grow and live in His grace. To know Him is to stretch my mind and heart, to be filled with His love and give it to those I meet. Why should I know God? He loves me in a way no one else does.

How do I meet God? I meet Him in friends and family who show me His love and care. They teach me how to let God be my friend and how to be a friend to God. They help me seek and find the truth. As we share our joy and our search for God as one body, I see God.

I also meet God when I am alone with Him. God comes to me through this Word as I read, through thoughts as I think. He comes to me when I seek Him as I fast and pray. I wait and God comes. I seek and God finds me.

I meet God in the Lord's bread and wine. Here He gives health to the sick, hope to those with none, and love to those who hate. Here, where we know His grief and our hearts are heavy, He changes the old ways for the new. He pours out His love to heal our ills, to give us hope and joy and to give us new life.

What do I do once I meet God? Jesus said, "Go and tell and teach." I live my life as one who has met the Living God and knows what it means to be loved.

Marigene Chamberlain

Through the
Looking Glass

Teeth brushed, face and hair just right. Now, one last peek in the glass. Okay, you look great, girl. But sadly, *I* know who you *are*."

Yes, I loathed me, but early as I can call to mind, my empty heart cried out to deaf human ears. Anger and shame took the place of hope. Cruel words, abuse year after year, and lies etched upon my soul an ugly image of who I am. I was my enemy. I didn't know how to change.

In my thirtieth year, a deep search for peace took me down a God-led path straight into the arms of the only One who could save me from me. For the next few months, my eyes began to open as Jesus showed me how *He* sees me, and through His Word and through prayer, I learned who I truly am. In Christ I am brand new, clean, and loved by God. I am His child…His bride…His joy…His own. For the first time in my life, my heart spilled over with true love.

To cling to Christ, to know God's love for me, and to know who I am in Jesus — these three are key. Each day I give God me, lift my hands to praise and thank Him, ask Him to mold and change me into the image of His Son, so that when I look in the glass, Jesus looks back.

We all, with open face beholding as in a glass the glory of the Lord,
are changed into the same image from glory to glory,
even as by the Spirit of the Lord.

2 Corinthians 3:18 KJV

Terry Magness

TO DROWN IN YOU

How long have You been in my life? All Time and a Day.

You began like a brook that flashed down the hill, clear and pure. In my first class in school, You were there as I ate lunch — gray, canned peas that sank in my white milk. When I sat on a cold school floor in first grade, You sat with me. You were with me as I tramped through the green field with my friend, Beth. 'strange that she was seen by You and me, but no one else.

Then Your brook grew to a river wide and splashed swirls of foam on rocks. You were with me at twelve when I cried, "I don't ever want to grow up!" And when I cried the night I wed, you were there. You have been with me in grave spots: when a car ran out of gas, when a job fell through, when a dear one passed.

All the while, Your mist began to creep into the nooks of my life — soft, damp clouds that took the edge from pain. You have been with me in a face, a song, a laugh, a tear. You have been with me in the pledge of a child, and you are with me still as I seek your help to raise him.

Now a sea, Your river has grown to a wide blue bay of wet warmth. You fill my mouth with words not my own; my eyes now see what once they did not. Though you have oft lacked me, not once have I been sans you, Lord.

Your waves crash 'round me until I am soaked. In You, I hope to drown.

Traci Stead

BOUND BY HOPE

The air was cold, and snow hugged my tires when I pulled up to the gate. Held to the gate was a fence that joined walls made of red brick, a large box that housed men who were knit heart to heart by a life of crime. Their lives — once filled with drugs, sex, and booze — now was filled with life in cells made of cold steel bars.

My charge from God was to serve these men, to be their friend in Christ, to love them as Christ so loved His church. They lived each day on the edge of death — at war with their minds, their hearts, their guards, and their God. My role with them was to bring a sense of peace — some calm in a storm — if only for an hour or two.

As I talked with these men, each one shared his hopes and dreams and prayed to live to see the day when his wife and child would hug his neck and love the man who once hurt them. They begged God to quell the cries of pain that once plagued their homes, and to let love flow once more. And so of course we shared about God and faith as each man hoped for a time that was yet to come. No doubt their plans would come true for them, as long as life and breath stayed in their lungs and hope stayed in their hearts.

Tim Wade

MAGGIE

Maggie hears my key go into the door. "Sniff" she speaks to the crack. She knows it's me. She jumps into my arms to greet me. "Lick, lick" lets me know she is glad to see me. "Take me out" is my dog's soft cry, as I reach for her leash. Like a free bird that is not free, she roams from tree to tree, then out to get the mail. She knows our trip in the yard well and goes through it with a bark or two.

When I first met Maggie, she was six weeks old and just a tiny ball of white fur, soft and sweet, with curls from head to toe. Early on, I took her out as I worked in the yard. I tied her leash to a tree so she could be with me as I put new plants in the ground. Very soon, I turned to see this little white pup with very black paws. She had dug in the dirt around the roots of the tree; and when I saw her, I could tell that she was thrilled to dig and play. I was not thrilled to have to bathe her, though. But I still smile when I think of how cute she looked.

MARTHA AND MAGGIE

At the time, I also thought, *That must be what God sees when He looks at us after we sin.* Just as soap and water cleaned Maggie, the blood of Jesus Christ cleans us. We have only to repent, and our souls will again be free of every spot. How great is our God! He knows what we need when we need it and will never leave us. "Thank You, God," I pray, "for your love and for my Maggie."

Martha VanZant

72
WHO CARES?

I want to care. I try, but I poop out fast. I watch the news and my mind reels. I scroll through Facebook, and I want to cry. I care so much I have to shut down. That feels wrong, so I pout and say, "Who cares?" To care seems the right thing to do, but to care BIG is too much. Maybe...just maybe I can care small.

A man with one leg sits by my bus stop. He holds silk roses made by his hand. He doesn't beg, but holds out a stem, smiles, and says, "For you!" I see him, and I care. Now and then I take a stem and give him five bucks. He gives back, "God bless you!"

Jesus said, "I was hungry and you fed me." He didn't say, "The world was a mess and you fixed it."

Did Jesus know an age would come when the glut of news could take over our lives, our minds, our hearts until we'd say, "Who cares?" Is that why He gave us such a basic focus? Food, drink, a roof, a coat; I can care for that kind of need. I can give to this one and that one from what the Lord has given to me.

I don't have to fix the Earth or my city or even my street.

To be sure, it seems that I don't have to *fix* at all.

I get to bless: The man with one leg; Louise, who needs a ride; Joey, who wants to talk; Edna, whose task is too big; my adult kids, who still need their mom.

Yes. I get to bless.

Bobbi Junior

PLAY TIME!

Once we hit adult age, we leave the ways of a child in the rear view. Yet, I miss play time when I was free to roam and find stuff in my yard and the woods of my small town. I still look for ways to play, even as an adult. Since I write and teach, I love to roam and find in the world of words.

My kids are part of my play world, as well, but often not of their free will.

On a given day, we might shop in a big box store. My son would stand on the side of the cart and — once I turned away — hop off and hide in the racks full of jeans or tops. I would turn back, and he was gone. I would call his name to no avail. Then began a wild hunt among the wares. After some time, he would jump out. "Here I am!" My panic would calm, but my stern words couldn't alter how much he loved to hide.

LORA AND SON, DAN

Some fun was in order. Tit for Tat.

The next time at the store, he began on the cart as usual. Then, he was gone. But I was ready. I didn't hunt for him. The store plays pop songs to shop by, and one came on that I knew. So I sang along at the top of my lungs, even off key for extra *umph*. I didn't care. It was play time.

I didn't have to wait long. My son arose from a rack with, "Mawwm!"

A little wit and a bit of tease saved my peace and his back side. He didn't hide again.

How do we seek God as a child? Add more play time, in all worlds.

Lora Homan Zill

74

CALLED TO BE SMALL

Please," I prayed. "Send me far. This place is too small to hold my dreams, to meet a man, build a home, serve You well, or gain much praise. Send me out to the world You made, that I may find the life You've planned for me."

"Stay," He said, in ten ways, and more. "Stay put. Dreams can be found even in small towns. This place, though well known to you, may hold a great prize you can't yet see, as you scan the globe for more."

I sighed.

He smiled. Laughed, I think, at my short sight, my poor hope, my lack of pluck, my warped range of view. "Keep your eyes on Me, child. I am where the road leads. In my great heart are fields, seas, stars, and worlds few can dream, and most don't find."

"It's not what I want, this place; this small, small scope, this hope no one else can see." I frowned.

"But, you love me, yes?"

"Yes."

"Then, stay."

I stayed. He grew my dreams; I wrote my heart. Those words flew and touched far-flung souls. Darts on a map mark their wide reach in His name.

He sent a man. We made a home. Served Him with full lives.

This "too small" place is now the launch pad for so much more — kids, books, prayers, art, life, my soul.

At first, I sought great things. When, at last, I sought the one great God, He gave me so much more. I dreamed of the world, but that first dream was far too small.

He knew, all the while. Hence, His smile.

Lori Roeleveld

CHRIST IN ME

Often folks try to put faith on like a shirt to wear to church, then change into comfy clothes when they get home. But faith isn't *on*; it's *in*: *"Christ in you, the hope of glory"* (Col. 1:27 NIV).

I can't leave Jesus at the door or piled on the floor. I can't shut Him off or screen Him out. I can't put my faith in a box while the rest of my life goes on.

I am the place He dwells, and He is holy, so all of my life is holy: every place I go and every word I speak. I work out with Him, and I veg out with Him. I plead with Him, and I praise Him. I write with Him, and — at times — I wring my hands with Him. He sees and knows all things.

Yes, Jesus dwells in every part of my life. With my kids, with my spouse, with my friends, with what I write, and even what I cook — may these all be His life in me. May I say what He wants me to say, go where He wants me to go, write what He wants me to write, and love how He wants me to love. May my life be built on Him and full of Him.

Like the old monk Brother Lawrence, I want to be aware of Him, my mind full of Him, at all times — until there is not one thing that is not holy in me.

To me, this is what "Christ in you" means.

Carole Sparks

FALLS AND TEARS

One day my child — my bright, busy, open child — will be grown. She will have put down many of the toys and tasks that fill her days and hours now. She will change. She will leave me, I guess, to walk on roads that may take her far from me. Up to now I've been able many times to choose the way for her; I have steered her to this or that course. At times she knew that I did, and at times I did it in the dark, so to speak, when she could not see my care.

ELIZABETH REDDING AS A CHILD

But the day will come when she will go where I can't reach out to guard and guide her.

It is hard for me to think that one day my child will be out there to stand in the stark cold on her own. She is so small and seems so frail at times. She trusts with such ease. The world is a warm place for her; it calls to her and she is free to come and should come — now. But when will she learn that some calls are best not heard? And how will she learn it? My guess is that she'll learn it through pain. She will be hurt. She will fall, or she will be pushed or even tripped by those who do not care for her as I do. There's a bright light in her eyes now and an easy smile on her face most of the time. Will these be wiped away by pain, washed away by tears? I wish I thought they would not. Or that I could take the tears and the falls for her. But I can't. The world isn't made that way.

So, for now, I hug her and tell her that I love her. I tell her that I'm here for her. She can come to me now, and I hope she will come to me then. I will not be able to hug away the hurts that the world hands out, and I don't think I ought to try if I could. The falls and tears will make her tough in ways that she needs to be tough. But when she is tough and grown and quite able to take the falls, I hope she will also still be able to take the hugs — and to give them as well, from that store of hugs that I add to as I can. I hope she will know that just as I was with her when she was a child, I am with her then. And one more hope: I hope that she will see my love as more than just mine, that as she looks back on and feels anew the warmth we share, it will make real for her the care God gives us all. I want her to see that it is God who cares for her, that God's great love comes to her through all those who love her.

And for me, I want to hold on to this truth: God will still do that even when she is far from my arms.

Mary Lou Redding

MARY LOU AND ELIZABETH, TODAY

HEART BLING

I admit it. I love bling — bright and shiny things to wear on my wrist, hand, ears, or neck. The ones made from real gold or fine gems are the best! Is it wrong to love bling? Am I vain or a show-off who wants my friends to envy me? Of course not. Sure, these things may cost good money, but they can also be quite cheap. The word *sale* is my friend, and only the store clerk needs to know how much I paid.

Each new item makes me happy…for a time. But then I begin to tire of it, and my smile begins to fade. *God wants me to be happy, doesn't He?* I think. So, off I go to the store for more. Home again, I take my bling out of the bag and hold it in my hand. Then I lift it high to catch the light. Oh, see how the jewel shines!

The best gems and gold have no flaws, but I am human and have so many. Only God can take *my* flaws — the anger, sin, scars, wounds, and hurts — and make my heart shiny and new again. As a child of God, I need to wear the things that show the world that I am His — love, joy, hope, faith, and trust. This is the bling that truly makes me *shine* from the depths of my soul.

> How much better it is to get wisdom than gold!
> And to get understanding is to be chosen above silver.
> Proverbs 16:16 NASB

JoAnn Durgin

Seeing the World through Short Words

If I could think to help re-ink a thought once tried and true
And in its place, wear on its face a short, blunt word or two

Where each bright word if read or heard speaks all it needs to say
In one swift punch and not a bunch, oh, how would be the way?

If I were smart and forced to start from parts this small and learn,
Would they all chop or flip or flop? Would they seem cold and stern?

Would words so brief press me with grief that it would tie my tongue?
Or would they spring a tune to ring and craft a rhyme that's sung?

For one swift beat can sound the heat of words like *singe* and *blaze*.
And leave me be with eyes that *see* when they could *glare* and *gaze*.

Oh, let me pine for gems to mine that cast their rays of hue
And words too large shall lose their charge when pearls yet small
shine through

And pierce the stone of verbs oft prone to length far past their prime.
For acts can *crush* stretched words to *mush* when pressed the least in
rhyme.

I'd be a fool to ban this tool far from my breath or brain
For words still short can quell the sort that hide in guise of "plain."

Then, let the earth burst forth the birth in pen and speech of lore
The life and flame to bid one's claim that small words hold in store.

Daniel Mynyk

ABOUT THE AUTHORS

Bob Adauto III (p. 51) leads a small group of men through addiction recovery at their church in Southern California. He's also a small-groups coach, leads a small group with his wife, and assists with the men's ministry. He's passionate about men's hearts and helping establish a better connection in their relationship with Jesus and their spouses.

Bob and his wife of 27 years have two adult children. He and his wife enjoy shopping at thrift stores, cooking, travelling, collecting things he doesn't need, and beautifying his saltwater aquarium.

Bob is the author of hundreds of police reports written over a span of 20+ years. He loves writing, painting, and drawing and hopes one day to have his own book on the shelf of a Christian bookstore.

Originally from a small farm town in Hayden, Alabama, **Sharon Atwood** (p. 56) earned a bachelor's degree in Language Arts Secondary Education at Birmingham Southern College. She then earned her Master's in Special Education at the University of Alabama at Birmingham and later became a certified Home Health Aide. She is employed by the National Alliance of Mental Illness. In addition, she volunteers with MPower Ministries preparing low-income adults with challenges to earn their GED.

Sharon immerses herself in poetry, writing, and artistic expressions. An active member of her local church, she enjoys participating in Bible studies in community settings.

At the end of the day, she curls up with her special baby cat, Kala Faith.

Joylene M. Bailey (p. 63) grew up on the Canadian prairies where rolling hills, just-mowed hay and the meadowlark's trill make her heart sing. She will always be a prairie girl at heart. Joy writes because. What began as making up childhood stories to put herself to sleep at night, became creating stories and songs for her three daughters. This entertainment morphed into writing articles and stories for children's publications.

Since then she has written short stories, poetry, songs, and devotionals. Her current work in progress is a novel about a wandering little girl and her flawed-but-loving mother. Joy hosts a merry and productive writers group in Edmonton, Alberta where she lives with her husband, daughter number three, and an impish cat named Calvin. She shares her joy-infused view of the world at www. scrapsofjoy.com.

Tandy Balson (p. 15) was born and raised in Vancouver, British Columbia, Canada. She and her husband now live on the outskirts of Calgary, Alberta. They consider themselves blessed that seven grandchildren — and their parents — live nearby.

Tandy's greatest joys include spending time with family and friends, meaningful volunteer work, time in nature, reading, and writing. She also gives a good foot rub — for which there's a long waiting list!

Tandy has been doing inspirational speaking in Western Canada since 2001. She is the author of two books, one of which was a finalist for the 2016 Word Awards in the inspirational book category. Tandy posts inspirational messages twice a week on her website blog and can be heard weekly on Hope Stream Radio: www.hopestreamradio.com/program/time-with-tandy/. Learn more at www.timewithtandy.com.

From the time she was a child growing up in Salt Lake City, **Trisha Barry** (p. 26) (pen name of Patricia Kittel) has lived by the adage "Service is the rent you pay for your place here on earth." Working for Muscular Dystrophy Association for 16 years, editing speeches for others, training high school students to be great public speakers, and teaching young people the love of reading have been some of her favorite ways to serve others. She's tried to instill her love for helping others into her three awesome grownup kids and her grandkids.

Pat loves writing poetry, commercial scripts, old-style letters, speeches, journals, even to-do lists — anything that involves writing. And while writing, she's found a cup of tea to be her best companion. It's always been the way she connects to ideas, friendship, laughter, and compassion. Tea and writing are passions she especially shares with her daughters and granddaughters.

Born into a family headed by an Army veteran father and a U.S. Navy nurse mother, **Jeff Brady** (p. 24) has always taken a keen interest in American History. That and his deep and innate sense of wanderlust have led Jeff to travel across most of America and live in each of the four contiguous time zones. He considers a great vacation to be venturing to an oft-forgotten historical marker that tells a story worth sharing, for, as Jeff says, "The path less taken often has the best stories."

Educated as a History Teacher, he spent a few years in the classroom and has since worked in industries ranging from videogames to music to textbooks. While those pay the bills, traveling our country and finding the "good" in his fellowman are his true passions — as shown in his frequent Facebook posts about "What Is Right with America" and his blog at www.wirwa.com.

Award-winning author and speaker **Tez Brooks** (p. 33) writes on marriage and parenting issues. Some of his work has appeared in *The Upper Room, Clubhouse, Focus on the Family,* Cru.org and CBN. com. His book, *The Single Dad Detour* was winner for the 2016 Royal Palm Literary Awards.

His screenplay *Jangled,* won 2016 Best Short Film at the Central Florida Film Festival. Other awards have been with Jerry Jenkins' Christian Writers Guild, Florida Christian Writers Conference, Blue Ridge Mountains Christian Writers Conference, and Florida Writers Association.

Tez is a mentor for Word Weavers International and a member of American Christian Writers Association and Florida Writers Association. He and his wife serve as full-time missionaries with Cru. They have four children and reside in Colorado. Read more about Tez at EverySingleDad.com.

David Buster, M.D. (p. 48) is a third-generation physician who retired from medicine in May 2017 after 40 years of practice including 25 in a rural ER. Along the way he formed friendships with his patients, mentored health-care students, and coached new physicians in their first years of practice.

He used to wonder why his old retired-dairy-farmer patients continued to get up at 3:00 A.M. long after they sold their last cows, but now, experiencing the wake-up call of his own retirement, he is beginning to understand just how hard it is to break old habits and to abandon the structure employment imposes on one's life. Today he spends his time reading, writing, being active in his church, enjoying the company of his family and friends, discussing health care with young family members now engaged in nursing and emergency medicine, and trying to teach fingers trained to probe for disease to find the chords on his guitar instead.

Kelly Carlson (p. 76) may live in the American Midwest, but she sometimes wonders if she should have been born in Africa — or at least in a place full of gratitude for simple things. Kelly enjoys sharing God's goodness through story, spending time with children, and Treasure-hunting for Christ's presence in the midst of the mundane. Three tools, she says, God has used to form her this way. First, His written Word and His Word — Christ, Himself. The second is her husband, Ben — steady and joyful, no matter the storm. And third is her daughter, Sophie Cait — smiley and adventurous, no matter the place.

Kelly is drawn to colorful, unique, and tiny things; to unexpected sincerity, sunshine, and sour candy. Severely struck by the Truth that she was bought by a King, Kelly strives to keep Christ first and to reflect the light of His tender heart in her life.

Marigene Chamberlain (p. 79) — Assistant Professor of Spanish at Samford University in Birmingham, Alabama — is deeply committed to helping students, faculty, and others develop their intercultural competency through living and studying overseas and through other cross-cultural opportunities.

She has much experience with people and places overseas both in her professional and personal life. She has lived and/or worked in Chile, Peru, Mexico, Panama, Ecuador, Venezuela, Brazil, Paraguay, Spain, France, Germany, the United Kingdom and China.

Prior to 2005, Dr. Chamberlain worked at the General Board of Discipleship, (a division of The United Methodist Church) in particular in the area of Hispanic/Latino ministries. She is the author of *Creer, Amar, Obedecer: El Discipulado Cristiano en la Tradición Wesleyana* among other books. She is also a translator and crossword-puzzle fan.

Alexander Chavers (p. 41) calls himself a "born writer" while acknowledging that there may not even be such a thing. Ever since he was three years old he's been telling stories. Imagination has always been key to his self-expression: so much so that he doubts that he could live without it. Currently he is a graduate student, originally from Cleveland but now studying communications in Washington D.C. In whatever his future career, he hopes to be able to tell a story, whether in the context of politics or creative writing — or maybe even both.

While working hard on his studies, he also makes time to blog, read, and write "the next great novel" that he hopes to publish one day. In his personal reading, he enjoys fantasy, science-fiction, dramas, and general fiction. Someday he hopes to write a novel in each one of these genres.

Jeanetta R. Chrystie (p. 77) and her husband live in Springfield, Missouri. She is a distance Assistant Professor of Business Administration at Southwest Minnesota State University. Jeanetta enjoys writing and has published more than 800 articles in magazines such as *Christian History*, *Discipleship Journal*, and *Clubhouse*. Her 150 newspaper columns appeared in the *Northwest Christian Examiner*, and she has contributed to anthology books and textbooks since the 1970s.

Jeanetta, a firm believer in spiritual journaling and prayer journaling, teaches Sunday School and has a passion to write Bible studies and devotions. As a survivor of both polio (age 2) and cancer (age 22), she clings to God as her mainstay and seeks to fulfill His reasons for preserving her life. Learn more about Dr. Chrystie at www.ClearGlassView.com. Connect with Jeanetta on Twitter:@ClearGlassView, LinkedIn: Jeanetta-Chrystie, and Pinterest: Jchrystie.

Lauren Craft (p. 36) believes our Heavenly Father gives each of His children a purpose, and that fulfilling His plan is one of the greatest joys we can experience before reaching our eternal home. God has blessed Lauren with a journalism post in Washington, D.C., where she has worked for ten years as a reporter and magazine editor. She has also been overjoyed to aid in Bible translation and share her hope in Jesus Christ on four continents. Her writings have appeared in the books *Just Breathe*, *Let the Earth Rejoice*, *Breaking the Chains*, and the magazines *Refresh* and *Living Real*.

Lauren lives in Woodbridge, Virginia and is happily married to Thomas Craft. You can connect with her at www.laurencraftauthor.com.

In 1994 **Jorja Davis** (p. 74) had minor surgery that resulted in major complications. Since then, she has learned that living with chronic pain that never lessens is clarifying, if nothing else. She no longer identifies herself by what she does but more by who she is and whose she is.

Once a classroom teacher, Sunday School coordinator, and youth director, she often has had to shift focus as her physical abilities lessen and the pain medication prescribed becomes stronger. Finally, in frustration, she went back to school for a second master's degree to prove to herself that her brain still worked.

As one door closed, somehow a window opened into new opportunities to serve. Jorja writes notes of encouragement and journals, blogs irregularly, and reads, edits, and reviews books. Jorja now focuses on supporting and encouraging her husband, children, and grandchildren. She is an award-winning writer and poet.

Through creative non-fiction, **Barbara D'Antoni Diggs** (p. 46) shares heart-touching God moments from her national and international experiences. For five years, she wrote a column for her church newsletter. She has written articles for *Contempo* and *Royal Service* magazines and guest blogged for *We, a Great Parade*.

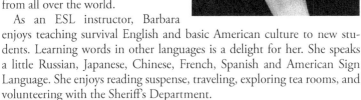

Barbara and her husband, James, live in East Tennessee. They have opened their home for over fifteen years to international students at Carson-Newman University. They now have children and grandchildren from all over the world.

As an ESL instructor, Barbara enjoys teaching survival English and basic American culture to new students. Learning words in other languages is a delight for her. She speaks a little Russian, Japanese, Chinese, French, Spanish and American Sign Language. She enjoys reading suspense, traveling, exploring tea rooms, and volunteering with the Sheriff's Department.

In 1999, **Jeanette Duby** (p. 35) moved to the Orlando area. There she began to see that God had been working in her life since she was a young child when a friend invited her to church. In that little Baptist church, she fell in love with preaching. She had never heard someone get so excited one moment and cry the next when preaching from the Word of God. Something touched her heart that day, and her life has never been the same.

It was several years later before she gave God her full devotion and really fell in love with his Son, Jesus Christ. Prior to this, she had been living however she wanted with no real direction, no passion, no real joy. Jeanette describes her life prior to knowing Jesus as "boring and lonely." She believed in Jesus Christ, but He wasn't her friend. She didn't have the *relationship* with Jesus she so thoroughly and intimately enjoys now.

Wendy Dunham's (p. 14) passion is writing stories that speak to the heart of her readers. Before she began writing children's books and middle grade novels; she spent years writing articles, columns, short stories, and devotionals. She strives to honor her creator with whatever she's writing about. Her stories share themes of hope, encouragement, and unconditional love — things we can all use a little bit more of.

She is the author of *My Name is River* (a 2016 Selah awards finalist), and its sequel, *Hope Girl* (a 2017 Saleh awards winner), both mid-grade novels for tweens.

When she's not writing, Wendy works as a registered therapist with children who have special needs. Visit her website: <u>wendydunham.net</u>.

A native of Indiana, **JoAnn Durgin** (p. 90) is a *USA Today* bestselling author of over twenty-five contemporary Christian romance novels. She earned a degree in journalism from Ball State University and then moved to Texas — where she met her husband, Jim, a ministry student at Dallas Theological Seminary. They have lived in California, Pennsylvania, and Massachusetts and now reside in Indiana where they enjoy spending time with their three children and first grandchild.

A former estate administration paralegal, JoAnn is best known for her Lewis Legacy Series as well as other popular series and standalone novels including *Catching Serenity, Heart's Design, Gentle Like the Rain,* the Wondrous Love Series, and the Starlight Christmas Series. JoAnn loves sharing God's grace and mercy through her novels. She can be contacted via her website at www.joanndurgin.com.

Nicey T. Eller (p. 42) grew up in the Florida Panhandle and decided she wanted to be a writer. She received her B.A. in English from Shorter College, and her M.S. in Secondary Education and Ed. S. in Educational Leadership from Troy University.

When she retired as an elementary school principal, she traded her suits for boots, built a log home with her husband, and started a cattle ranch.

Her poetry, inspired by teachers, has been published in *Teachers of Vision* magazine. She was a co-author of *The Mighty Pen (Christian Encouragement from Writers to Writers)*. She serves as a Sunday School teacher and leader in Celebrate Recovery. She is an avid reader, walker, and letter writer. Her contact information is nicey.eller123@ gmail.com and facebook.com/nicey.eller.

Sherree G. Funk (p. 45) belongs to an army of water warriors dedicated to bringing clean water access to millions of people around the world. World Vision, with its excellent staff and committed donors, aims to end the world water crisis by 2030. Sherree and her husband, as members of World Vision's National Leadership Council, love to share what they saw in Ethiopia when children turned on a clean water tap for the first time. Their joyful faces were unforgettable.

Sherree's teen Bible studies on Lydia, Joshua, Ruth, Peter, and Hannah highlight characters who faced problems not so different from those of today's youth. She teaches groups of young people at her churches in Pittsburgh, Pennsylvania and New Orleans, Louisiana. Her studies are available on her website, ServingOneLord.com and on Amazon.

Steve Garnaas-Holmes (p. 11) is a United Methodist pastor in Acton, Massachusetts. He has also served in New Hampshire and Montana. For 37 years, he wrote and performed music and comedy around the country with a quartet called The Montana Logging and Ballet Co. But everybody kept laughing at them so they quit.

Steve writes worship songs and other resources and also writes "Unfolding Light," a daily reflection at unfoldinglight.org.

He lives with his wife, Beth, a spiritual director. They have three grown sons and two grandsons who he says are beautiful enough to convince you of the evidence of evolution in two generations. He begins every day with a morning walk in the woods and is always looking for someone to play Frisbee with him.

Desiree Glass (p. 71) has written for numerous publications and websites including *Guideposts, Christian Devotions,* First Place 4 Health's national e-newsletter and holiday devotional *A Joy-Full Season, Pen in Hand* (Maryland Writers Association publication), *Connections (*College of Southern Maryland literary magazine), *Dragonfly* (HopeWorks of Howard County magazine), *Element Connection* (Potomac Ministry Network blog), *The Times-Crescent* newspaper, and her church blog.

Currently a career-and-technology-education teacher at Chopticon High School, Desiree has 30 years of experience teaching ages from infant to adult. She earned her B.S. at Salisbury University and her M.A. at Notre Dame of Maryland University. She is the mother of three children and grandmother of eight. In addition to spoiling the grandkids, Desiree enjoys photography, hiking, and life on the farm. Desiree's blogs can be read at http://desireeglass.blogspot.com/.

Writing has been a part of **Pamela Groupe Groves**' (p. 57) life since her fourth grade teacher introduced her to writing creatively. The *Short and Sweet* request for fictional works motivated her to finally write a story inspired by her Grandma Myrtle whom she knows little about except that she died in 1941 when Pam's mom was twelve.

Pam's life perspective was shaped during childhood when God taught her that every life is different. This background prepared her for teaching, moving with her husband from Oregon's high desert to the coast, and finally the big city while parenting six adopted children, four with special needs. Their life was a little offbeat with challenges and unexpected twists and turns, including her husband's death at age 62 from a rare form of cancer. Through it all, they trusted that God was present with them through all they faced.

Lydia E. Harris (p. 67) enjoys spending time with her family, which includes two married children and five grandchildren aged 7 to 18, prompting her to write *Preparing My Heart for Grandparenting: For Grandparents at Any Stage of the Journey.*

She has also contributed to 30 other books and has written hundreds of articles, devotionals, book reviews, and personal-experience stories for dozens of publications.

With a master's degree in Home Economics, she creates and tests recipes with her grandchildren for *Pockets* and *Clubhouse* magazines. She also pens the column "A Cup of Tea with Lydia," which is published across the U.S. and Canada and has caused her grandchildren to dub her "Grandma Tea." She also speaks at writers' conferences and community events. Lydia and her husband, Milt, live in the Seattle area and recently celebrated their 50th wedding anniversary.

Leah M. Hinton (p. 61) has been fascinated with words since she first learned to read as a precocious four-year-old. She never ventures out into the world without a book or two in her bag and dozens more on her phone. After all, she reasons, what better way to combat the lull of almost ceaseless carpool lines?

Leah and her detective husband have been together for nearly thirty years and have two wonderful teenaged children, a son, 15 and a daughter, 17. She rounds out her family with five rescue dogs, a bird, and a rescue horse — all named after her favorite characters in literature.

Leah writes both fiction and non-fiction and is fueled by highly caffeinated coffee and a never-ending faith in God. A country girl at heart, this homeschool mom and cancer wife loves sharing her struggles and blessings with others going through similar situations and firmly believes that faith is the best remedy for life's toils. Find out more about Leah at authorlmhinton.com.

Paul Aaron Hinton (p. 59) is the son of a proper British mother and a Mississippi mud father. Never sure if he should aspire to be James Bond or a character from *Hee Haw*, Paul has worked in many "fields."

He hopes his colorful — if not ADD — view of the world reaches those who have never been sure if God needs them. Thus, Paul's motto is Philippians 4:13: *I can do all things through Christ who strengthens me.*

Paul has served the Methodist church for over 20 years as a Lay Minister in both youth and contemporary worship.

He and his wife, Cecily, have three children, plus a "Crazy Cat Lady" starter pack of four cats and two very big dogs.

Becky Hitchcock (p. 72) is a judicial secretary and has lived all but six months of her life on the family farm located in Old Clyattville, a community outside Valdosta, Georgia. She and Keith, her high-school-sweetheart husband, have two daughters.

Becky has always been fascinated with the written word, but she did not give writing a priority until her second brother passed away. Whether penning articles and prayers or piddling with a work of fiction, Becky feels God smiling when she writes. She would rather write than talk. When not writing, she reads about writing and writers. She still finds time to bake an occasional pound cake, walk a beach, and collect vintage Blue Willow china.

Over the last twenty-five years, **Shauna Hoey** (p. 78) has developed curricula and workshops, led support groups, and taught elementary school. After Shauna's home burned in 2012, her experience inspired her to share tools to help others recover after trauma and loss. She authored *Fire of Hope: Finding Treasure in the Rubble* and developed ThriveWithHope.com which provides resources, encouragement, and connection with others who survived trauma and learned to thrive and even flourish after trauma.

Shauna is married to her best friend and soul mate, Rex. Their blended family of six amazing children and three grandchildren, fill them with love beyond measure. They live in Manitou Springs, Colorado with their youngest son and their King Charles cavalier dogs.

Visit Shauna's blog at ThriveWithHope.com.

Katherine Kavanagh Hoffman (p. 65) lives and writes in Edmonton, Alberta, Canada. A transplanted Montrealer, she has also enjoyed living on the west coast, where she studied at Regent College, Vancouver, B.C., and received her Master of Christian Studies (1990). Some of her favorite people include her husband Kent, her two grown daughters and their partners, and her little granddaughter Elizabeth.

Kathy is a member of Inscribe Christian Writers' Fellowship and a current columnist for *Fellowscript* magazine. She enjoys participating in Writers' Café, a local writers' group, and credits her fellow members with encouraging her to step out of her writing comfort zone. Kathy considers life an adventure, and tries to live it with that attitude. She occasionally blogs about it at This Life is an Adventure! kgehca.blogspot.ca.

Marlene Houk (p. 18) writes a series of Bible studies titled *Backstage Pass to Bible Women.* They connect ancient women to us, conveying messages of hope, faith, and warning.

Marlene is passionate about finding the Master Director's heart prints in the women He has positioned in His Word. And she loves to ask unusual questions such as, "What one word did Eve omit in her conversation with the devil?"

She writes for the *Blue Ridge Christian News* and encourages women through her teaching and speaking ministry. Her Bible study, *Backstage Pass to Emotion Commotion,* won first place at the 2016 Blue Ridge Mountains Christian Writers Conference.

Marlene is a graduate of Covington Theological Seminary with a degree in Ministry and Gardner-Webb University with a degree in Business Administration. Learn more about the fascinating world of Bible women at www.MarleneHouk.com.

Charles J. Huff (p. 66) served as a Bible teacher and minister in his church for twenty years. He and his wife have traveled three times to the Philippines where they held pastors' seminars and taught in various churches.

He is a contributing author to James Stuart Bell's *Gifts from Heaven: True Stories of Miraculous Answers to Prayer* and his devotionals have been published at www.christiandevotions.us and *The Upper Room*. His Boosterclub blog at www.chashuff.wordpress.com offers encouragement toward the abundant life Jesus promised. He and his wife are charter members of Word Weavers International of Aurora, Illinois.

When not writing, Charles can be found out in nature with his camera or working on his list of chores and errands. He and his wife live in Aurora, Illinois, near their five children and six grandchildren.

Penny L. Hunt's (p. 60) greatest desire in life is to help others enter into a passionate relationship with Jesus Christ. She is an award-winning Amazon.com bestselling author, speaker, devotions writer, and posts a weekly blog, "A Thought from Penny." The wife of a retired naval officer and attaché, Penny shares with warmth, motivation and humor the life lessons she has learned on a journey that has taken her from the east coast of the USA to Hawaii, Europe, South America and back.

Penny's adventure continues as a grateful grandma, happily living among the peach orchards of rural South Carolina with her husband Bill, and Hunley, a rescue dog from the streets of Charleston. Penny is a prolific writer and member of Word Weavers International. Visit her at her website www.PennyL.Hunt.com.

Connie Inglis (p. 73) lives in Edmonton, Alberta, Canada. As a long-term missionary with Wycliffe Bible Translators, she has spent much of the last 25 years in Southeast Asia with her husband and children — serving as a literacy specialist, teacher, and editor. Since 2009, Connie has been posting her poetry and blogging about overseas living and has seen both her poetry and short stories published.

She is passionate about Jesus and seeing Him in day-to-day happenings, about family — particularly her grandchildren — and about art, in all its forms. She views her recent trip to Europe as life-changing, especially her visit to the Van Gogh museum in Amsterdam which she considered her #1 bucket-list item.

Jeanie Jacobson (p. 17) is on the leadership team of the Wordsowers Christian Writers Group. Her writing shares hope, humor, and godly encouragement. In addition to her book, *Fast Fixes for the Christian Pack-Rat*, she's published in the best-selling *Chicken Soup for the Soul* series, *Focus on the Family* and *LIVE* magazines, and various anthologies.

Although married to Jake, the only perfect man in the universe, Jeanie's in the midst of a love affair. (Since it's with Jesus Christ, Jake is fully on board.) Jeanie enjoys visiting family and friends, reading, hiking, and gardening. She's passionate about helping people become organized, bringing order from chaos. She's involved in various ministries at her church, Bible Truth Ministries, including the praise dance team. Connect with her on her website, JeanieJacobson.com or at facebook.com/JeanieJacobsonWriter.

Linda Jett (p. 12) wrote, worked in the area of healing massage, and lived out her dream on the Oregon Coast with her husband of thirty-seven years. A member of Oregon Christian Writers, her true stories appeared in a variety of collections including anthologies by James Stuart Bell and Donna Clark Goodrich and *Guideposts*. Her work also appeared in *Just Us Girls* Chicken Soup for the Soul, *Kaleidoscope of Life* (a collection of poems), several LIVE magazine publications and *Bible Advocate* magazine.

She also authored and contributed poems to various organizations. Her published book *meggelsprout* (a children's book) was a finalist in Cascade Writing Contest in 2013.

Linda passed away on March 8, 2016, leaving this world for a better world — one she loved to talk and write about.

Bobbi Junior's (p. 84) memoirs depict difficult times juxtaposed with God's faithfulness. Life has provided her with challenges in caregiving, disability, abuse, and mental health. Bobbi's passion is to use story to show how the Lord brings about value for our suffering. She lives with her husband of 30+ years and their two dogs in Edmonton, Alberta, Canada and has two grown children. Visit www.bobbijunior.com to explore some of her award-winning memoirs and download a chapter of *The Reluctant Caregiver* and her short story, *Tell Me About Today*; and read or download *When the Bough Breaks*, posted in its entirety.

Bobbi works as a Communications Coordinator for a Human Services group and sits as Chair of her church board. She also serves on the executive board for InScribe Christian Writers' Fellowship (inscribe.org) which hosts a writers' conference during the fourth weekend of every September.

In the summer of 2017, **Tom Kennedy** (p. 34) retired from Houston Baptist University as a professor of psychology and counseling. He taught marriage and family courses as well as human sexuality at the undergraduate level. In addition, he was the chair of the Master of Arts in Christian Counseling program where he taught Christian integration of Bible, theology, and counseling. Tom has been a Licensed Professional Counselor in Texas for almost thirty-five years. Due to hearing loss, he has retired from face-to-face counseling but continues to work as an email suicide crisis counselor for Global Missions Online.

These days, Tom is busy playing with six grandchildren and trying to start a writing career. Prior to his teaching at Houston Baptist University, Tom and his family were missionaries to Japan for fourteen years.

Liz Kimmel (p. 47) and her husband of 38 years live in Minnesota and have two children and four grandchildren. She earned a BA in Elementary Education at Bethel College in Arden Hills, Minnesota.

She is a writer and layout editor for her bi-monthly church publication. Liz has published two books of Christian poetry and loves to write in such a way as to make learning fun for elementary students. She has published a grammar workbook, and her current project is a set of worksheets about the 50 U.S. states — created in order of statehood and incorporating math and language arts skills, in addition to lots of puzzles. Liz currently serves as the communications coordinator for her church, Bethel Christian Fellowship, in St. Paul.

Rita Klundt (p. 54) is a wife, mother, grandmother, nurse, and storyteller. When she's not at her day job doing cardiac research, she enjoys blogging, motivational speaking, and laughing with family and friends. She loves a good mystery, creating rhymes, home-style cooking, and traveling with her husband, Roger. They make their home in central Illinois, where they serve through their local church by leading youth in Bible study and fun activities.

In her memoir, *Goliath's Mountain*, Rita offers a glimpse into the hearts and minds of hurting people. She tells a passionate, poignant and tragic story, but in her writing and in her life, God's faithfulness gives her hope, helps her find purpose in spite of pain, and brings out the downright funny when it's needed most. Rita speaks, not as someone who has arrived, but as someone who has been there. Contact Rita at www.wetfeet.us or www.goliathsmountain.com.

An energetic high school student with a zest for life, **Adrienne Large** (p. 28) has many interests in the world surrounding her. From sports to baking, and photography to gardening, she enjoys adding an artistic flair to all that she does.

When Adrienne first heard about the opportunity to submit a poetry piece for *Short and Sweet, Too,* she enthusiastically accepted the challenge of creating a poem within the syllabic restraints of the book's established guidelines.

Her foundation for poetry and love of fine writing has been built by reading classical works from Lord MacAulay, Samuel Taylor Coleridge, and her personal favorite, Emily Dickinson. Adrienne is committed to glorifying God with her pen through poetry as well as children's fiction.

Note: Because Adrienne is a minor, her photo has been withheld at her parents' request.

According to her husband, **Julie Lavender** (p. 19) has trouble telling the short and sweet version of a story. Julie loves details and more details, but she likes to think that makes her an attentive interviewer.

She freelances for newspapers; writes for *Guideposts Magazine*; authored *365 Days of Celebration and Praise, Creative Sleepovers for Kids,* and three teacher resource books; and contributed to *Chicken Soup for the Soul* compilations and magazines such as *Today's Christian Woman, Focus on the Family, Mature Living, Country Woman, ParentLife,* and *Taste of Home.*

Julie is married to her high school and college sweetheart, David, and is mom and mom-in-law to Jeremy, Jenifer, Jeb Daniel, Jessica, and Adam. Follow the former public school teacher and homeschooling mom at julielavender.blogspot.com.

Marcia Lee Laycock's (p. 70) work has been published in magazines, newspapers, and anthologies in Canada and the U.S. and appears frequently on the world wide web. She writes a regular devotional column, "The Spur," which appears in publications across Canada and goes out by e-mail to avid readers. Marcia's writing has won many prizes, garnering praise from notable Christian writers such as Janette Oke, Mark Buchanan, Phil Callaway and Sigmund Brouwer.

She has published four devotional books, five novels, and many short stories. Marcia won the Best New Canadian Christian Author Award for her novel, *One Smooth Stone.* The sequel, *A Tumbled Stone* was short-listed for an award along with her fantasy novel, *Journey to a Strong Tower.* She is a sought-after speaker for women's events. To learn more about her, visit her online at www.marcialeelaycock.com.

Mary Elaine Lester (p. 53) is a writer/actor/storyteller from Little Rock, Arkansas. Mary seeks to inspire and entertain with her stories. She believes that if we can pause and look up from painful circumstances with a breath of hope, then God will be there: "*I will lift up mine eyes unto the hills, from whence cometh my help*" (Ps: 121:10). After many weary miles of driving through the southern Alabama flatlands, Mary looked up to see that hills had appeared. From those hills came her inspiration for *Hope on the Wing*.

Mary has performed stories for Tales from the South, a syndicated radio show. She enjoys movies, singing, and collecting wonderful moments and then sharing them with friends. Mary is working on her first book, a collection of "looking up" stories, *Love God and Wear Sunscreen*.

Connect with Mary at amaryvoice@gmail.com and maryelainelester.com.

Terry Magness (p. 80) is a licensed minister and founder of Grace Harbour Ministries, established in 1995 as a Biblically based teaching and discipleship ministry. Her experience as a pastoral counselor and Bible teacher has enabled her, through Ever Increasing Grace seminars and workshops, to help many people struggling with life issues. Her travels in ministry have taken her to many countries in the world where those same principles for victorious living in Christ have been effective in changing lives.

Terry's books, *Ever Increasing Grace* and *Azadiah Reynolds: God's Jamaica Man*, encourage readers that no circumstance in life is beyond God's grace to heal and overcome. Currently, Terry mentors class leaders, develops curriculum, and teaches and facilitates classes for the Overcomers Ministry she established in her local church.

Jill Allen Maisch (p. 68) and her husband, a United Methodist pastor, live in Damascus, Maryland. For decades, most of Jill's writing consisted of creating labs and engaging activities for her seventh-grade science students. More recently, she has been encouraged to develop a gift for writing short devotions that share how different experiences helped her recognize God's very real presence in the world and strengthened her faith.

The piece in this book was written after her first attempted devotion was nearly critiqued to death during her first writers' conference. Later during that same conference, though, Jill's confidence as a writer developed and she began to hone the skills necessary for quality writing. She is both humbled and blessed that five of her devotions have since been published in *The Upper Room* magazine.

Chantel Mathson (p. 27) has traveled all over the U.S. and parts of Canada, speaking and inspiring others to become impact makers. She has been a keynote speaker, workshop facilitator, breakout session leader, fashion show host, and emcee, featured in marketing campaigns and involved in numerous charitable special events.

As a college professor, she seeks to always find the best in every student and to help him or her achieve his or her own potential for greatness.

Chantel leads Bible studies and has created women's groups in several states that inspire and empower women to become leaders. As a military wife, and mother of three, Chantel has experienced the impact of moving a lot. This has led her to a lifelong commitment to creating communities to support others and to spread joy and laughter in the world.

Joy E Miller (p. 37) lives in Virginia. She has written devotionals for *The Upper Room*, christiandevotions.us, and Focus on the Family's *Odyssey Adventure Club*. She has also been published in the magazine, *Reach Out Columbia*. Her true story, "The Day the Brick Wall Fell," was included in the book, *The Extraordinary Presence of God*, compiled by Ann White Knowles.

Joy enjoys ministering to people by writing encouraging letters. She is passionate about the lives of unborn babies and helping to equip their parents. Volunteering at her local crisis pregnancy center is a privilege and a joy. Above all, she revels in being an aunt to Anna and Patrick.

Alice H. Murray (p. 55), a proud member of a military family, lives in Florida where she has practiced adoption law (domestic non-related infant adoptions) for over 25 years. Alice is an officer and board member of the Florida Adoption Council and of Hope Global Initiative.

While being a lawyer is her profession, Alice's passion is writing. Alice has written articles for legal professional magazines as well as for her local paper and a missions' magazine; she also won an American Bar Association haiku contest. Alice had a non-fiction piece published in *Short and Sweet* (the first book in the *Short and Sweet* series). In the near future, she hopes to have two books published — one a humorous devotional book and one a look back at her career as "Boss of the Babies" doing adoption work.

Daniel Mynyk (p. 91) is a software engineer who loves to think deeply and apply himself critically. With a limitless thirst for truth, Daniel enjoys breaking down complex subjects into simple concepts. His most important passion is to love and serve Jesus Christ, desiring to know Him more each day. He relishes every opportunity to serve in church by teaching classes for adults. His other interests include systematic theology, apologetics, philosophy, politics, economics, linguistics, technology, and martial arts.

Daniel holds a B.S. in Computer Science from Pensacola Christian College and an M.S. in Information Systems from the University of Phoenix. He is the author of the book *Freedom to Give: The Biblical Truth About Tithing* and the owner of the budding apologetics website TruthHub.org. He lives in Colorado with his wife Chelsea and three children Aiden, Brody, and Elianne.

Suzanne Dodge Nichols (p. 40) grew up in Gulf Breeze, Florida. During high school, she discovered the rewarding discipline of writing. Through the years, she has found creative expression in almost every genre of the printed word. She enjoys blending words and art in ways that can both delight and challenge the observer.

Suzanne leads a scripture-memory and Bible skills program for older elementary children. Her many years as program director led her to develop a three-cycle curriculum for older children. More recently, she added a companion curriculum for younger elementary children — a foundational program she named "Bible Basics."

Suzanne makes her home in Hartselle, Alabama with Roger, her husband of 41 years. They have three children and seven grandchildren who live much too far away.

Shelley Pierce (p. 39) is a pastor's wife, mother to four, grandmother, and author. Playing with the grandkids is her favorite way to spend a day. She also enjoys her day job, serving as Director of Preschool and Children's Ministries at Towering Oaks Baptist Church in Greeneville, Tennessee.

Her writing includes children's curriculum with *LifeWay Kids*, a column in *Christian Online Magazine*. She has contributed to *The Upper Room, Power for Living, Guideposts The Joys of Christmas, The Mighty Pen*, and *Stupid Moments*. Her middle grade novel is titled *The Wish I Wished Last Night*.

Shelley chooses to look at the bright side of life, believing that God can be trusted to keep His promises. To her, difficulties in life — such as a son deployed in a war zone — are all opportunities to grow in faith and depend on God to meet needs. Check out her weekly blog at shelleypaperbackwriter.blogspot.com.

Judy Webster Powers (p. 75) is a Christian wife, mother, grandmother, author, publisher, and retired registered nurse. She is from northern Alabama, having lived most of her life in Hartselle. Married to Dan Webster for 28 years, together they raised three children. During this time, she compiled and self-published *The Chocolate Lovers Cookbook* and *Chocolate and More*. Combined, the books sold over 7,000 copies.

Dan lost his battle with cancer in 2007. Judy married John Powers in 2011 and now makes her home with him in Andalusia, Alabama along with their two dogs Buster and Brelee. Together, she and John have six adult children and ten grandchildren. Judy continues to be an avid chocolate lover and enjoys quilting, crocheting and writing.

Sandy Kirby Quandt (p. 64), an inspirational writer with a passion for God, history and travel — passions that often weave their way into her stories and articles, is author of numerous articles, devotions, and stories for adult and children publications, including two compilation books of nature and dog devotions,

Sandy has won several awards for her writing including the 85th and 86th Annual *Writer's Digest* Writing Competition, First Place in the Blue Ridge Mountains Christian Writers Conference Children's Literature 2016 Foundation Awards, and First Place in the 2017 Foundation Awards in the Young Adult, Middle Grade, and Flash Fiction categories. Check her blog, *Woven and Spun,* for words of encouragement or gluten-free recipes. You can also find her at *Inspire a Fire* and *Christian Devotions.*

Anne Foley Rauth (p. 13) grew up in a small town in Northwest Missouri, with a high school graduating class of only 44. After high school, Anne received her MBA from the University of Kansas and immediately went to work at Hallmark Cards in their Advertising and Hallmark Hall of Fame division. She also worked at other Fortune 500 companies such as H&R Block managing national promotions and sponsorships but ultimately followed her passion and is currently working in the nonprofit sector.

Anne belongs to the Heart of America Christian Writers' Network, and has led sessions at their annual conference. She has also spoken at the Wordsowers conference in Omaha, Nebraska.

Anne and her husband Scott have 3 boys, live in a house that was built in 1909, and have a dog named Abbie the Labbie. Anne would love to connect with you at arauth@annerauth.com.

Mary Lou Redding (pp. 88-89) earned a degree in English Literature and a graduate degree in Rhetoric and Writing. After teaching basic composition and writing for pre-professional majors on the college level, she came to work for the international daily devotional magazine *The Upper Room*, for which she taught at writers' conferences nationally and internationally. The assignment that led to the essays in this book grew from the effective writing workshops she taught for colleagues.

Several years ago — after thirty-three years with *The Upper Room* — she retired from her position as Editorial Director. In retirement, she has rediscovered the joys of having free time. She loves being more available to her family, especially in being part of the early years of a surprise grandchild. She is working on her eleventh book in a meandering, grandmotherly sort of way and dreaming about her twelfth.

Linda Jo Reed (p. 20) is a writer with a mission: to glorify God and encourage His people. Her message is that life's battles belong to God and that He will see us through them when we stand firm. His promise comes through Isaiah 41:10: that we are not to fear, that He holds us in His hand. In *Upheld In the Battle*, Linda Jo's first book, she illustrates these very things.

Linda Jo is currently working on another book, and her writings have been published in *Evangel*, *The Upper Room*, *Good News Northwest*, analogies, and blogs. Her own blog can be found on her website: www.lindajoreed.com. She lives in the Pacific Northwest, is grandmother to nine boys and is owned by two cats.

Reba Rhyne (p. 52) is the pen name of Reba Carolyn Rhyne Meiller. In high school, reading was a favorite past-time. More than once at 1 A.M. she would hear, "Carolyn, turn off your light and go to sleep."

Three-quarters of a century have passed since Reba was born. During this time, she was married for 25 years, had a daughter, and established a business of her own. Writing began as a hobby while she spent months at a time at her customers' locations. She now travels the world for pleasure and business.

For sixty years, she has been a Christ-follower who believes that her responsibility is to live out the Great Commission found in Matthew.

She shares fifteen acres in Tennessee with Phil the Groundhog, skunks, possums, rabbits, squirrels, deer, an occasional bear and her cubs, a high-flying hawk, and a bobcat. They get along very well.

Susanna Robar (p. 21) grew up in southern California. After graduating from local schools and the University of Redlands, she married Robert L. Robar. Robert, now retired as a Los Angeles City Fire Captain II, and Susanna, retired as a Spanish teacher, have five children: two with the Lord and three adult children, and four grandchildren — all of whom live in southern California.

Through Susanna Robar Ministries - *RapeSpeaksOut!* and written instructive materials, workshops, seminars and short-term courses, she delivers presentations that educate concerned groups — parents, teachers, pastors and other child caregivers — about sexual violence, child safety, and human sex trafficking. The goal is to help heal victims of sexual violence, and teach pro-active prevention tactics for all children.

In 2013, she received the Inaugural Cottey College Alumnae Hall of Leadership and Social Responsibility Award because she has "demonstrated exceptional leadership and exemplified selflessness for the good of others."

State and national award winner **Janet Ramsdell Rockey** (p. 25) is a freelance writer in Tampa, Florida. Her writing survives the demands of her full-time job as a legal secretary, her part-time job in real estate, and indulging her precious feline "children." These diversions inspire her to write stories published by *Chicken Soup for the Soul* and many short devotions in Barbour Publishing's various collections.

She has authored two 180-day devotionals: *Discovering God in Everyday Moments* and *Fear Less, Pray More*.

Janet is a member of Florida Writers Association and past president of Word Weavers, International – Tampa Chapter. Her critique groups keep her focused as she carries out her calling to spread God's word through her writing. See her blog at: Rockeywrites.blogspot.com.

Lori Stanley Roeleveld (p. 86) is an author, speaker, and disturber of hobbits who enjoys making comfortable Christians late for dinner. Biblical, funny, and real, she inspires courage and Christ-centered confidence. She's authored three non-fiction books including *Running from a Crazy Man, Jesus and the Beanstalk*, and the upcoming, *The Art of Hard Conversations*, as well as a Christmas novella, *Red Pen Redemption*.

Though she has degrees in psychology and Biblical studies, she learned the most from studying her Bible in life's trenches.

Blogger. Wife. Mother of adults. Part-time giant-slayer. Not available for children's parties. Though she has tried to escape, she still adventures with Jesus in a small town in Rhode Island. To join the adventure, knock on her door at www.loriroeleveld.com.

After dabbling in several careers throughout her adult life, **Dottie Lovelady Rogers** (p. 32) is now happily retired. She is a graduate of Huntingdon College, Scarritt College, and the University of South Alabama. She was blessed to spend twenty years in the areas of local church Christian education and university campus ministry. She then had many rewarding years as a professional counselor in several settings.

She now enjoys hanging around the house with her husband Ken and their dog Shep. They live near the gulf coast where gardening is a twelve-month project. She also loves to read, cook, write, and teach adult Bible study. After fifty years of discipleship, she is still learning to follow. Although a reluctant disciple, she is always amazed at God's grace and guidance.

In 2003, **Pamela Rosales** (p. 30) joined a writing group and then Oregon Christian Writers shortly thereafter. She began writing freelance and her articles, poems, and devotions have been published in several Christian publications since 2004. Some of the publications include: *The Secret Place* and *God's Word For Today* devotionals; *Live*, a Gospel Publishing House leaflet; June Cotner's poetry anthology books; and *Imago Dei* magazine.

Pamela has worked as an administrative assistant in public schools, in her church, and as administrator for her husband's court-reporting business. She has also served in various leadership roles in her church and as a women's Bible study leader. She and her husband have entered a new phase of life and now spend retirement half their time in Oregon and the other half in southern California.

Carol Schafer (p. 22) is the author of three children's storybooks: *Lorenzo's Incredible Leap: A Story of Courage*; *Grison, the Grumpy, Grouchy Island Goat: A Story of Healthy Choices*; and *Cloddia's Desert Dance: A Story of Finding Your Place*.

Carol worked as an academic editor for twenty-seven years, editing undergraduate course materials in a wide variety of disciplines. She now volunteers her editing skills with InScribe Christian Writers' Fellowship (www.inscribe.org).

In addition to writing and editing, Carol spends her time

sewing, playing bass guitar, tending backyard flowers, reading, cooking, loving her family, and serving in her church. Carol is a children's advocate for Compassion Canada and sponsors children in several countries. She is also the founder of Destiny Dresses, a sewing ministry that creates beautiful dresses for little girls. Find Carol's Facebook pages at Carol Schafer Author/Editor and Destiny Dresses.

Deborah Brawer Silva (p. 23), a messianic Jew, is also a published science writer and technical editor. She and her husband David, once a UCLA linebacker, teach "The Jewish Roots of Christianity," a Bible study class they developed for their church. Deborah and David are working on a Bible study guide that features topics covered in their classes.

They have two adult children. Their daughter is a chemist, and their son is a computer programmer. Both are believers. Here's the "rest of the story" after Deborah initially told David to find somebody else to

date, David replied: "But I like you. You're one of God's chosen people. Jesus died and rose again for you, too. The first Christians were Jews." Deborah's Uncle Louie became a Jewish Christian when he was 81 years old after several all-night Bible studies with David.

In full-time ministry for over 40 years, **Neil Silverberg** (p. 29) has served as Senior Pastor, Bible teacher, author, and cofounder of Masterbuilders, an organization that provides leadership training and church oversight to a network of New Testament churches throughout the U.S. His Jewish heritage as well as his dedication to Biblical study contribute to his unique ability to illuminate the Old Testament as the basis for understanding the New. He is a father to four generations of pastors and church leaders through his one-on-one discipling and mentoring.

Neil is the author of four books including *For Truth's Sake: Restoring a Passion for Truth to the People of God* and *From the Fold to the Flock*. He continues to write books, blog, and record new teaching. He is a gifted musician and has recorded two music albums; *Deep Calls to Deep* and *One New Man*, both containing songs he has written.

Lynn J. Simpson (p. 58) understands the need for creating spaces and tools for rest, renewal, and transformation. She loves to facilitate retreats for spiritual formation, and coach people on stepping into their dreams, visions, and goals. She writes stories to inspire hope, and rarely is without a camera in hand to capture breathing spaces to share.

Her first publication, *30 Day Journal of Thankfulness, Successes, and Joy* has been used by individuals, groups, and ministries to help develop new mindsets. Her latest journal, *Breathing Spaces, a 21 Day Journal of Rest, Reflection and Renewal,* features her photography from the Canadian Rockies to the deeper south of Savannah, Georgia. Lynn resides in Sherwood Park, Alberta, Canada. However, you'll often find her on the road, discovering new scenic places God has created.

Born in 1923, **Fay Henry Smith** (p. 31) grew up on a farm in Central New York, but his eye was always on the sky. After graduating from Ohio Wesleyan and Drew Theological Seminary and his appointment to a parish in Farmingdale, New Jersey, he was delighted when a parishioner offered him free pilot training and the use of the airport facilities.

Later he and his wife, Sally, answered the call to missionary work. They established the Wings of Caring aviation service in Zaire (now Democratic Republic of the Congo). Upon retirement, Fay worked with United Methodist Men in Nashville, Tennessee until his death in 1991.

Carole Sparks' (p. 87) list of former roles continues to lengthen: architect, minister's wife, overseas worker, and ESL teacher. Although she doesn't claim these titles any more, each still colors her perspective on the world. Carole now finds her freedom in the hills of East Tennessee where, alongside her husband, she writes (and revises), runs, and raises her children.

With a Master of Arts in Theology, Carole is passionate about God's Word and how it can change our everyday lives. She likes to approach Scripture in unexpected ways and dig into familiar Bible stories until she finds something fresh. That's why she has written devotions and Bible studies for various print and on-line media. Look for her new Bible study series, *Dwell*, coming soon. Check out Carole's blog at http://notaboutme1151.wordpress.com or connect with her on Twitter, Facebook, and Instagram.

E.V. Sparrow (p. 50), writer and illustrator, enjoys sharing life with her new husband and young grand-children, and also being a caretaker. Her favorite activities are hiking, kayaking, drawing, and painting.

E.V. has led prayer teams and small groups in Divorce Care, Women's, and Singles' Ministries. She sang in several choirs and with a worship team. E.V. has lived abroad, served in the mission field, and traveled extensively.

Short stories of freedom, hope, and love written by E.V. are *Meaghan O'Meara's Bowl,* and *Don't Bypass Joy, My Love. Ella's Heart,* will appear in the 2017 Inspire *Love* anthology.

E.V. was a muralist and her illustrations appear in *Little Known Tales in California History.* She is a member of Inspire Christian Writers and the Society of Children's Book Writers and Illustrators.

Traci Stead (p. 81) has been married nearly thirty years. She and her husband are West Virginia natives, but now call North Carolina home. They have two grown sons who are their pride and joy.

Traci has been a teacher for many years, including home schooling her own children through their entire school experience. In addition, she has made a business out of teaching home schooled children the joys of writing and literature. She now reaches across the ocean to teach English to children in China.

Traci writes inspirational fiction as well as devotionals and Bible studies. You can read her weekly blog at www.TraciStead.com and also read about her latest releases.

Traci enjoys hiking, reading, and traveling. She also likes British television series, though she admits to not being able to understand half of what they say.

Susan Reith Swan (p. 69) is a writer from suburban Pittsburgh, Pennsylvania. In addition to writing for the Christian market, she is also passionate about writing for children — anything from picture books to YA, fiction and nonfiction — and for five years was the editor of the children's magazine *Story Friends*.

At her church, she is a women's small-group Bible study leader and sings in the choir. In her spare time, Susan enjoys reading, knitting, and doing crafts of every kind. She is the mom of two grown children, a boy and a girl, and lives with her husband, Tom, and a Cavalier King Charles Spaniel, Phin, who is the real head of the house.

Tammy Van Gils (p. 16) is dedicated to planting words and growing stories that bloom with hope. She is a thriving survivor of abuse, abandonment, and adversity. How? By the Master Gardener›s grace, the Vine›s love, and the Advocate›s renewal — emotionally and spiritually. She is sowing life with Henry, her husband of 35 years, a Yorkie Poo named Moose, and a dozen chickens. Her life harvest includes two sons and four grandsons. She enjoys gardening, quilting, and writing.

Tammy is a member of the American Christian Fiction Writers. She›s honored to be a guest blogger and also a contributor to *The Wonders of Nature Devotion Book* and *So God Made a Dog*.

Culitvate a connection with Tammy by subscribing to her blog, *Writing Hope for the Everblooming Life*, at Tammyvangils.com.

Martha VanZant (p. 83) has lived in central Florida for most of her adult life. She made her living as a dental hygienist while raising her family and still works part-time at this profession that she considers a ministry rather than a job. Her six siblings also reside in the area, and together with the rest of her very large family, they afford her much material for writing.

Martha is involved in church work and volunteers in the church bookstore regularly. She attends Bible studies for spiritual growth and socializing. In her semi-retirement, she enjoys writing short stories and devotionals, reading, photography, and spending time with her family. Time alone with the Lord each morning and in her garden give her the quiet time outside with nature that allows for ideas for writing to surface.

Beverly Varnado (p. 43) is an award winning novelist, screenwriter, and blogger. In addition to ten years working in the fashion industry, two years directing a ministry, and nine years home schooling her children, she has also been involved in many volunteer efforts including as a United Methodist Church lay speaker, board member for the University of Georgia Wesley Foundation, and a participant in the Athens Symphony Chorus.

Her screenplay, *Give My Love to the Chestnut Trees,* has been a finalist for the Kairos Prize and is now under option with Elevating Entertainment Motion Pictures. Her novels are *Home to Currahee* and *Give My Love to the Chestnut Trees,* which placed in the top ten for Christian Writer›s Guild Operation First Novel.

Her blog, *One Ringing Bell,* is now in its seventh year with almost seven hundred posts. Her work has been featured on World Magazine Radio, *The Upper Room* magazine, and *Southern Distinctions Magazine.* Learn more at www.BeverlyVarnado.com.

Tim Wade (p. 82) is a husband, father, grandfather, author, chef, former college pastor, and former volunteer prison counselor. His passion is to feed people in both body and soul. To this end he founded Dinner with Dignity, a grass-roots ministry that works closely with homeless shelters and other organizations to provide restaurant-quality meals for people marginalized by society.

Tim has written for *Deeper Devotion*, an online magazine for high school and college students, *Christian Devotions*, and Focus on the Family's *Clubhouse Magazine*. When not working, Tim enjoys spending time traveling with his family. Among his many passions, he especially enjoys touring old towns and cities where he learns about their food, culture, and history.

Margery Kisby Warder (p. 44), author and speaker, has taught Bible studies, written curriculum, and presented church and community programs. She worked for newspapers before buckling down to complete two novels, an original Christmas collection, a busy woman's instant retreat book, and a children's Advent book. She also co-authored devotionals with her husband, Paul. Her 11 books are available on Amazon.

In 2016, her poem about Abraham's journey up Mt. Moriah won first place at OWFI and earned her a 2017 scholarship to Mt. Hermon Christian Writers Conference. Since then, she's begun making her poetry available on canvas — accompanied by photography or artwork — as the Third Glance Series. Margery also conducts "Publishing on a Dime" workshops. To learn more or to contact her, email her at author.speaker4Him@ gmail.com or follow her blog at https://margerywarder.wordpress.com.

Kenneth Avon White (p. 49) is an aspiring writer whose work was published for the first time in *The Upper Room* magazine. Ken's professional background includes work in radio and television advertising, public relations, corporate communications, and most recently, information technology. He dreams of the day when he can make writing his career; but in the meantime, he is grateful for the clock he punches.

Ken currently resides in Nashville, Tennessee and enjoys the local music scene, theatrical shows, and art exhibits. Also high on his list is dining out with a cast of characters — otherwise known as close friends — who have all been warned that most likely they will find themselves in one of his stories someday.

Lora Homan Zill (p. 85) is a teaching artist with the Pennsylvania Council on the Arts and an adjunct instructor at Gannon University. Her award-winning poetry and nonfiction have been published widely, including co-authorship of a chapter in the textbook *Teaching Creatively and Teaching Creativity*. She edits and publishes the Christian literary poetry journal, *Time of Singing,* and teaches at arts, education, and writing conferences.

Lora founded Blue Wind Artistic Retreats to honor creative expression as an act of worship and a way to feel God's pleasure in our lives. She is working on a book about how creative expression leads us to deeper intimacy with God.

Lora is a musician on her church worship team and is creating a series of small stained glass windows for its sanctuary. She is currently completing a commission of wildflower images in stained glass. She blogs on creativity, faith, and the arts at www.thebluecollarartist.com.

SUSAN CHEEVES KING

Susan Cheeves King has worked with *The Upper Room* magazine for over 22 years. She has also taught English and feature-writing classes for over 27 years, serving at Lipscomb University, Biola University, and Abilene Christian University.

She has served as book editor and radio-program producer/on-air talent for The Institute of Scriptural Psychology, written magazine features as a freelance writer, and functioned as a seminar facilitator in leadership and group dynamics.

Susan and her husband, Joe, have three grown children and two young grandchildren.

CPSIA information can be obtained
at www.ICGtesting.com
Printed in the USA
FSOW04n1605101117
40841FS